Myron Lee
and the
Caddies

Rockin' 'n Rollin' Out of the Midwest

by Myron Wachendorf
with Chuck Cecil

Enterprise Books • Brookings, South Dakota

Copyright © 2004
by Chuck Cecil

ALL RIGHTS RESERVED
This work may not be used in any form,
or reproduced by any means,
in whole or in part,
without written permission
from the publisher.

Library of Congress Control Number: 2004108407

Hard Cover ISBN: 1-893490-09-2
Soft Cover ISBN: 1-893490-10-6

*Published by
Enterprise Books
1036 Parkway Blvd.
Brookings, SD 57006*

First printing 2004

On the cover...
The cover photograph is a scene from the 1961 first-ever coast-to-coast tour of Canada by American rock and roll artists. Myron Lee and the Caddies made the tour at the invitation of singer Buddy Knox. In Montreal, the Caddies played for over 10,000 enthusiastic Canadian fans. From left (back cover) to right (front cover) are Jerry Haacke, Cal Arthur, Myron Lee, and Randy Charles.

Printed in the United States of America
PINE HILL PRESS
4000 West 57th Street
Sioux Falls, SD 57106

*For my wife Carole,
and for Bob and Jillania Wachendorf
and their children Samantha and Ethan;
daughter Kelli and husband Dave Laughlin
and children Danielle, Ryan, Austin, and Baylee;
and son Kris Wachendorf and Leslie
and their daughter Megan Spears Wachendorf.*

Table of Contents

Foreword vii

Introduction xi

Chapter One
An Early Death 1

Chapter Two
The Family Survives 9

Chapter Three
A New Sound in Popular Music 17

Chapter Four
Help Is on the Way 27

Chapter Five
On the Road 43

Chapter Six
On to Flin Flon 49

Chapter Seven
Bobby Vee Opens Doors 63

Chapter Eight
Dick Clark's Caravan of Stars 71

Chapter Nine
Another Clark Tour and a Death in Dallas 81

Chapter Ten
Rocky Road for Rock and Roll 87

Chapter Eleven
Stepping Back and Moving Forward 99

Chapter Twelve
Ballrooms, Street Dances and New Year's Eve 111

Chapter Thirteen
The Last Dance 131

Epilogue 139

Caddies through the Years 141

A Veteran Caddie Remembers 142

Myron Lee Discography 144

1963 & 1965 Dick Clark Caravan of Stars Tour Schedules 145

v

Foreword

Remembering Myron Lee

By performer, actor, and recording star Bobby Vee

It was late summer in 1963 and I had just returned from a calendar of bookings in England. I still had several weeks of gigs in the upper Midwest and I was looking for a local band to back me. In a casual conversation with Jimmy Thomas, Myron's agent, I discovered that Myron might be interested in doing the dates. He had backed Buddy Knox for a while and had a fine career of his own. Although we had never previously worked together, the word was he had a tight band and was willing and able to travel.

I drove from Fargo to Sioux Falls, SD, to rehearse with him in his basement studio. When the band was set up he kicked into a rockin' version of "Hello Josephine" and before he finished the first bridge I knew Myron and the Caddies were the band I was looking for. All were excellent players. The lead guitar player, Curt Powell, was exceptional, one of the best in the Midwest and a great guy. He was big time quirky but lived to play. Myron was a heartfelt singer and a great band leader.

We toured that fall throughout the upper Midwest. The following spring, newly married, my wife Karen traveled with me as I toured the continent, France, Italy, Holland, and back to the UK. Back in the U.S. we hooked up with Myron and company once again and worked the entire summer, ballrooms, lake pavilions, armories, and amusement parks...south to Oklahoma...southeast to Florida where Karen and I spent our off days basking in the sun and being in love. It was a great time in our young lives as we played a series of shows up and down the Florida coast. In spite of being a couple of months pregnant with our first son, Karen was able to hang in with the gang while we all went deep sea fishing. And in spite of being so seasick, she managed to land the most fish. Red fish and shark...she out-fished us all...

Not long after that short tour I was booked to play the "Teen Fair of Texas" in San Antonio. It was a week long Texas "tent" event—hot...and Texas humid...a few degrees cooler than fire and like many of the shows in the early days it featured both rock 'n roll and country acts (George Jones). It was also one of the first shows that the Rolling Stones played in America and because of the new sounds that were coming from England. Yeah... yeah.... yeah...there was much anticipation of their performance. I still remember their introduction—and the screams—as the master of ceremonies announced the act, followed by silence as they walked on stage with their amplifiers, plugged in, and began to tune. After several minutes they slipped into a Birmingham (UK) version of "Walkin' The Dog". The mostly country/pop audience stared at them...as my friend Johnny Tillotson would say..."like a herd of cows looking at a new fence." Interestingly, Myron's sax player on that tour was a Texas boy by the name of Bobby Keys. Along with Bobby's great innate talent on the sax he got on famously with all the Brit lads and lo and behold...a short time later became a mainstay in their touring band as well as playing on many of their most memorable records. With humor and great affection Keys recounts the San Antonio show in Bill Wyman's book.

During that summer run, Myron and I became good friends and it was clear to me that he was the glue that held the Caddies together. They were all good players but he was the pivot point, the go to man. He treated them with great respect and they in return followed his direction. Because of his ability to motivate his players he became one of the best band leaders around.

Somewhere along the way I received a call from Dick Clark to take part in a Caravan of Stars tour. Because very few acts carried bands and because Myron made it all seem so easy, I recommended to Dick that he hire the guys to back the entire show. Dick agreed and we proceeded to play thirty some shows traveling from eastern Canada to central Texas and all points in between. Business was great and by mid November, we had gone full circle, right back in Texas with the Dick Clark Caravan. While it was getting ready to snow up north in the Dakotas we traveled across Texas through an all night rain storm arriving at the Dallas Sheraton around 9 a.m. I was in bed and sound asleep at 10 a.m. when Brian Hyland called my room and asked if I wanted to see the president. "Kennedy's gonna be in a parade," he said, "and it's going by close to our hotel."

I took a pass and later he and Myron showed up at my door one more time. I gave my camera to Brian and some cash to Myron and slept until around 12:45 p.m. when Myron called again to say that Kennedy had been shot. Unbelievable! President Kennedy....shot dead! What I remember most is the flag across the street from my hotel room flying at half mast...and later the stories about Jack Ruby watching the same TV screens as we were in the lobby of the same hotel. My only frame of reference around this tragedy was the February 3, 1959, plane crash that took the lives of Buddy Holly, Richie Valens, the Big Bopper, and young pilot Roger Peterson enroute to Moorhead, MN, from Clear Lake, Iowa. Having met with the remaining acts after they arrived for the show, KFGO, the local radio station in Fargo, decided that the show must go on and asked for local bands to help out. I was fifteen years old at the time. Holly and the Crickets were my favorite group and I was full of mixed emotions...should we play...should we not. It was the night that my career started as a fill in band called the Shadows. President Kennedy's death brought back all those hollow, lost memories.

Back in Dallas I was once again numb...dumb...and in shock. The Dallas mayor, or someone, closed the town while they searched for the gunman (Lee Harvey Oswald). Unlike the Winter Dance Party tour...I learned that night that the show doesn't always go on.

I'm not sure that Myron would agree but for my money he was the Midwest king of rockabilly. He had the moody look, the energy, and the attitude. Listen to "Rona Baby" and tell me that he wasn't born too late. He was drawn to the same music...the same time period...the same rockin' stuff that every Sun Records fan understood...the stuff that didn't need fancy words...the stuff that just made you feel good. It's what Myron was all about.

Nor Va Jack Studio in Clovis, New Mexico, is where Buddy Holly and the Crickets recorded their greatest hits. Myron traveled from Sioux Falls to Clovis to record several of his records...it's what he loved...that's where his heart was. He made some terrific records, well produced, well performed...and maybe just slightly out of step with the emerging pop market. While the Five Satins were singing "In The Still of The Night" Myron was writing rockers like "Homicide." Maybe if he had rewritten "Rona Baby" ten more times he would be a living legend...like Link Wray. Maybe if he had started a few years earlier he would have been touring the main circuit with Gene Vincent, Jerry Lee Lewis, Johnny and Dorsey Burnette and maybe Paul Burlison would have been the "hot" picker on his records. Don't get me wrong...he was a good rocker and I always thought he deserved more. Anyone who's ever met Myron would agree that he's a great guy and I felt honored when he and his wife Carole decided to name their son after me. He disarms people with his quick wit and even in the early years was quick to speak his mind. As it happened, he enjoyed a great career close to home, close to his family. He had a great following of fans and could have played forever. His band days only came to a close because he decided it was time. Until that day arrived, he played his heart out and had one of the best bands, always, anywhere! And...you only have to hear the opening refrains of "Rona Baby" to know that he was a home grown rockabilly kind of guy.

I have a lot of Myron stories. Like the time I got arrested for having an open beer can (10 of them) under my passenger seat...hey...I was Myron's passenger! He had no idea!!! I paid a fifty buck fine and I can still hear Myron laughing.

Then there was the time that Myron accidentally left me behind after a show at Maple Leaf Gardens in Toronto. I was chatting with a custodian and waiting for him to finish packing his gear when I saw Myron's car's tail lights leave the building.

There was the time he was late for one of the Dick Clark Caravan of Stars shows. Myron thought he had plenty of time to make the early show but overlooked a detour and the slow moving winding roads of West Virginia. As the band finally arrived and set up...Dick talked to the audience nonstop for at least 45 minutes. What a trouper!

One time Billy "Summer Time" Stuart sat in on drums with the band...the drum stool folded under his large frame and he disappeared under the backdrop. Billy played all the way to the floor as Myron looked on wide-eyed. There was nothing but a pair of feet sticking out from under the curtain.

The time...the time...the time...so many great times...and great memories about a great friend...Myron Lee...the rockabilly cat!!!

Introduction

Myron Robert Wachendorf, known professionally as Myron Lee, was the first rock and roll talent to catch the public's ear and the people's notice in South Dakota in the late 1950s. He is considered to be the "founding father" of rock and roll in his native state. While still in high school in his hometown of Sioux Falls, the natural musician and born showman organized a band made up of his Washington High School classmates Jerry Haacke and Barry Andrews, along with Dick Robinson, who was a student at Augustana College in Sioux Falls, and Curtis Powell of Garretson. They called themselves "The Caddies" and began to perform locally, attracting full houses and happy Sioux Falls crowds at the Stardust Club and later at the Cabana Club.

The Caddies had their first out-of-town date in 1958 at the Tyndall Groveland Park Ballroom, playing during the breaks taken by the featured group known as Moller's Accordian Band. Over the next thirty-four years, Myron recorded thirteen single records and three albums. Many of those first recordings were written by Myron, including "Baby Sittin" which was also recorded by an English group known as Bobby Angelo and the Tuxedos. It became a big hit in Europe in 1961, and royalties for the song are still being sent to Myron. Many of his records are now much sought after collector's items.

The professionalism and style of the group of young high school students that played in Tyndall in 1958 appealed to all ages. Before that historic night at the Groveland Park Ballroom was over, the dance hall manager, George Beringer, having observed the excitement and audience appeal that Myron Lee and the Caddies created during their brief intermission performances, hired them to come back the next Saturday. The word was out and the group was soon in great demand throughout the upper Midwest.

Since he can remember, music has been a part of Myron Robert Wachendorf's life. Before moving from Parker, SD, to Sioux Falls, Myron's father, Bob Wachendorf, had a popular Parker-area band. It played all the small towns in the area, and a small notebook Myron still has lists the dates, places, and payment Bob received, such as "Feb. 1, 1938, Hurley, $2," or "Jan. 30, 1940, Sioux Falls IOOF, $3.00." After getting a job at Weatherwax Men's Store in Sioux Falls, Bob quit the Swingsters and became a pick-up musician for area dance bands in the late 1940s. Often, he took young Myron along on his local gigs.

Sometimes, he called his five-year-old son to the stage to join the band. Young Myron sang and played the drums. His dad also taught Myron basic piano cords and urged him to sing loudly for the customers at the Grange Avenue Barber Shop while young Myron was getting his locks trimmed by barber George Everetts on Saturday morning. He was particularly good at singing the WW II song, "Pistol Packin' Mama," made popular by the Andrew Sisters.

Myron caught the rock and roll fever while attending the 1955 movie *Blackboard Jungle* at the Hollywood Theater in Sioux Falls, and hearing its theme song "Rock Around The Clock" by Bill Haley and the Comets. The song is considered by most music historians as the beginning of the rock and roll era which captured the nation until the invasion from Britain of The Beatles in February 1964.

As a sophomore in high school, while attending a Teen Hop at the Arkota Ballroom in Sioux Falls, Myron crowded up close to the stage with other teenagers, enthralled with the music of Sonny James as he sang his number one hit, "Young Love."

That was the impetus he needed. He decided he'd become a professional musician like James. Until then a piano player, he taught himself, with help from Jerry Haacke, to play rhythm guitar and formed the Caddies. Myron Lee and his music became an instant hit in Sioux Falls. His stage presence, honed while watching his father perform, and by appearing before audiences since he was old enough to walk, helped make him and his band a favorite to tens of thousands of fans. Over the next three and one-half decades his music and style were a part of the musical scene in South Dakota, the upper Midwest, and throughout North America.

He dropped out of school in May of his senior year to pursue full time his dream out on the dance circuit, traveling a five-state area with his fellow Caddies. They played in barns, dancehalls, taverns, high school auditoriums, hockey rinks, night clubs in communities big and small, and even in supermarket parking lots. His Midwestern fame soon caught the eye—and the ear—of some of the nation's top recording stars of the day, including Buddy Knox, Bobby Vee, and many others.

Myron Lee and the Caddies toured Canada coast to coast with Knox and later traveled the nation with his good friend Bobby Vee of Fargo, ND. He and Bobby often appeared on the same billing at dances throughout the United States.

The Caddies' big break came when they were recommended to Dick Clark by Bobby Vee, and Clark of ABC's *American Bandstand* booked them to be the back-up band on the Dick Clark Caravan of Stars in 1963. As part of that cavalcade, Myron Lee and the Caddies performed in dozens of American cities with a Hall of Fame cadre of the nation's biggest stars in music. So impressed was Dick Clark with the professionalism and talent of Lee and his fellow Caddies that when he organized the 1965 Caravan of Stars, he didn't hesitate to invite the Sioux Falls group back.

"A remarkable facet of the Caravan of Stars was the backup bands," says Clark. "They had the chore of providing the music accompaniment to the fourteen or fifteen acts that appeared on stage. One of the all-time best was Myron Lee and the Caddies. Myron ran a tight ship, and we're all indebted to him for providing the musical spine for our stars."

"Talent, followed immediately by reliability," remembers Clark. "Myron has them both. He's always had guys that can play. He is the epitome of reliability. I've been extraordinarily lucky in picking people (for the tours) that know their stuff. I figured he knew what he was doing, and fortunately my amateur appraisal of him worked out very well."

Mention Myron Lee and the Caddies in the upper Midwest and people older than thirty-five immediately shake their heads in response and smile when they say they remember the group and the good times dancing and listening to Caddies music that was mostly rock and roll and rockabilly, but sometimes drifted to country music, too.

In 1992, Lee unplugged his Fender amp, closed the case to his black, hollow-bodied Gretsch guitar that had survived Canadian cold and Miami heat, and called it quits, ending a truly remarkable music career. In 2001, in recognition for his contribution to the upper Midwest music scene, he was inducted into the Iowa Music Hall of Fame. He was only the second non-Iowa resident to be selected for the honor. The previous year, Buddy Holly was inducted posthumously. In 2000, Myron received a lifetime achievement award from the Minnesota Rock Country Hall of Fame.

In the pages that follow, Myron recalls his years on the circuit, cutting records and running with the big names in the business. He shares his disappointments, the ups and downs of being in a tough business, and his fond memories of the thousands of road trips over literally hundreds of thousands of miles through all kinds of weather that the Caddies took traveling from one performance to the next.

This courteous, polite, somewhat bashful, high school dropout with an ear and talent for good music is arguably the best known rock and roll performer to ever come out of the state of South Dakota.

This is his story.

1

An Early Death

It was one of those slate-gray Dakota days. The chill in the air was the last gasp of a long winter retreating north. A cold drizzle softened the remaining banks of pitted snow that had drifted in around the headstones, and the mist brushed the smooth granite grave markers that were so tall they seemed to press in all around me.

Clouds scudded along on the stiff March wind over the little country cemetery just north of Marion, SD, known as St. Mary's Catholic Cemetery. The low clouds brought everything down to my eight-year-old level. I stood next to my mother, my sister Marlene and brother Marv, and wished that I were somewhere else.

His casket was suspended over the newly dug grave that had been chiseled through the frozen ground the night before. My dad, Robert Wachendorf, was being buried. It was 1950. I looked north to the small farmstead shrouded in the mist. My dad had been born on a farm, and attended St. Mary's Catholic Church when he was a boy my age twenty-five years before. He was baptized in St. Mary's Church in 1917, a good boy of German stock whose parents spoke with a Low German accent. And now he was in this forbidding place forever. I could come back and see his grave whenever I wanted. I silently promised him that I would.

My mother was crying softly. All of my aunts and uncles and Dad's many friends were standing around the grave, heads bowed, as the priest said the last rites. I bowed my head and glanced out of the corner of my eye, to my brother and sister nearby.

Now, so many years later, I can still see that cemetery scene and the dim outline of the farm buildings out near the cemetery. And I often wonder how my life might have been different had he lived longer. Would he have allowed me to drop out of school and leave home with that small rock and roll band I'd put together that became known as Myron Lee and the Caddies, playing in all sorts of places to all manner of people? Or would he have insisted I finish high school and go to col-

1

Bob Wachendorf, Myron's father, who died when Myron was eight, instilled in his son a love of music, and nurtured Myron's musical talents.

lege? I think he would have reached out, tousled my hair, and encouraged me to follow my musical pursuits. Yes, I think he would have gotten a kick out of seeing Myron Robert Wachendorf up on stage doing what he, too, so loved to do.

Music had been a part of my life since I can remember, thanks to my dad. I guess it was because of some mystical convergence of the dynamics of parent and child. I seemed to have inherited a musical aptitude from my father's side of the family. Of the three Wachendorf kids, I was always the one to reach for Dad's arm, begging him to show me how our old upright piano in the dining room worked. He'd gotten me started early with his impromptu, after-work lessons of the F sharp cords at home, and on the drums at the Melody Dance Hall in downtown Sioux Falls, SD. When he took me for my haircuts before I was five, he'd hoist me up on the padded kid's board angled across the barber chair arms, and encourage me, with the added urgings of George and Dean Everetts at their Grange Avenue Barbershop, to sing the songs he had taught me. And although I was shy, I sang anyway. I suppose it was to please my dad. I think he wanted me to know the joy of song and melody, and I was fortunate to have inherited some of his musical talents.

So I believe he would have been proud of what I was able to accomplish during that exciting time of change in the 1950s and 60s when rock and roll music rushed through the door. It replaced the mellow-voiced big band crooners like Frank Sinatra, Vaughn Monroe, and Perry Como; and the new sound nudged the exuberant, bouncing fox trotters of WW II times over to the slow lane to make room for the heavy beat and fast-moving rock and roll beat. Rock and roll music was born in the mid-1950s, fathered by Bill Haley with his "Rock Around the Clock." It marked an historic change in American music. I wanted to emulate the sound of Bill Haley and the Comets, and I decided to do it the way my dad would have wanted me to do it, in an honest, professional manner with the sincere attempt always to entertain people in a tasteful style.

My life started early in the morning of June 24, 1941 in Parker, SD, a small town southwest of Sioux Falls. I was born at home, in our house rented from Archye Beaumont. Being born at home then was still a fairly common occurrence in a rural area with no hospital within a half-hour's drive. There was neither time nor money for that, so a country doctor came by our house and assisted my mother Alice while my dad entertained older sister Marlene, who was then five.

Six months after my birth (I was the second of three Wachendorf children) our family moved to Sioux Falls. My father, up until then, had been a part-time laborer and handyman. He found needed work during the 1930s with the federal-state Work Porgress Administration (WPA) making furniture. But he also spent a good share of his time playing in bands. He was blessed with an uncanny ear for music. Often at wedding parties, anniversaries, Saturday night dances, or an evening at the VFW Club, the pay for "Bob's Swingsters" came out of a hat dutifully passed before the evening's last dance, which traditionally was "Good Night Sweetheart."

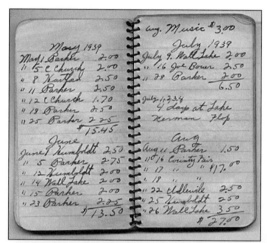

Myron's father Bob, also a musician, kept a small note pad record of his appearances at dances and other events where he helped provide the music. Here is his record for May through August of 1939. He wrote that on May 12 he played at the Catholic Church and received $1.70. In August, he played three days at the Turner County Fair and made a total of $17.

Myron's father Bob Wachendorf, far right, and his band in the Parker-Marion, SD, area in about the mid-1930s. Jack Vogt is one of the sax players, along with two men whose last names were Unruh. Levi Guemmer played the bass violin, Delbert Church was on piano, and Bernie Pfuffer was the horn player.

The times were tough and money was scarce. Often, the passed hat might complete its round trip back to the stage with only a few dollars and some loose change. The money was split among the musicians, and it helped each of them buy some of life's necessities. But the Bob Wachendorf family still struggled to make ends meet.

In Sioux Falls, he began working in the mailing room at the newly opened Army Radio School. The school would eventually attract 40,000 young men through the war years, so one of the by-products of their presence was a proliferation of lounges, dance halls, and ballrooms in town, and they flourished for a time.

At one time in the late 1940s to the mid-1960s, there were as many as eight nightclubs out on West Twelfth Street, which is now Highway 42 west of Sioux Falls. The lineup of clubs started at Twelfth and Kiwanis, which at the time was, for some reason, called "Screwball Corner." From Screwball Corner, clubs were sprinkled all the way to the Tea/Ellis road two miles down the highway. To comply with local laws, they were all "bottle clubs," where the customers brought their own bottles of liquor and then purchased their mix from the club.

Those clubs had entertainment every night of the week except Sunday. When the bars in town shut down at midnight, a good share of the customers headed west where the clubs remained open until 3 a.m. I remember that the 7 Oaks was a real hot spot where I played years later when I got my band together. The Flamingo Club was another popular watering hole and featured big pink flamingos made of wood, all standing on one leg, up on the roof, spotlighted for the night. It was hard to miss the Flamingo Club. When I was about twelve, my mom took me there to see the great black piano player Hobs Mason, who was a Flamingo regular for years. I was facinated by his piano talents and could watch him play for hours. Looking back now, I think he sounded a lot like Joe "Fingers" Carr, who had several hit records at that time. But I digress.

In Sioux Falls, Dad, who had quit his band in Parker, joined with three other self-taught musicians to play as a pick-up band. They were in demand and could have been booked every night of the week had they wanted to. Sometimes he worked in pick-up bands with Myron Floren, until Myron left Sioux Falls to join the Lawrence Welk band. Dad could play both the accordion and the piano, or any instrument if he set his mind to it. He'd never had a music lesson in his life.

This was all at the tail-end of a long Depression made even more difficult in a rural state like South Dakota because of the ravages of dust and millions of hungry, munching grasshoppers and crickets that ate everything in their paths and then tried wooden posts and shovel handles for dessert. But in the 1940s, as the air base at the Sioux Falls Airport expanded and brought more GIs in for aviation radio training, the pain of the Depression soon passed. People were returning to a somewhat normal life that had been interrupted by the hardships of the Dirty Thirties. It was wartime, of course, so it wasn't exactly all milk and honey, but economically speaking, things were different in Sioux Falls and for our little family.

As the war heated up in the world, I am certain that my dad was disappointed to learn that because of a genetic happenstance, he could not serve his country. Doctors discovered that one of his legs was slightly shorter than the other. He was classified

4-F. Despite his misfortune, I don't recall that he walked with a limp, so the problem must have been slight.

I was too young to have a clear memory of the war years 1941 to 1945. But in the late 1940s, as our family's fortune's slowly improved, I remember that my dad got what he thought was a plush job at the Weatherwax Men's Store on Phillips Avenue in downtown Sioux Falls. At that time, incidentally, the city had seven motion picture theaters, all within six blocks of one another. There was The Time, The State, The Egyptian, The Strand, The Granada, The Orpheum, and The Hollywood. All of them had matinees and evening shows, so in my growing up years I sat through hundreds of movies. I was especially fond of the cowboy movies of the day, and Roy Rogers was my hero.

Myron, about two years old, and his sister Marilyn, about seven.

By now, Dad had quit the Swingsters, but he had gained enough local notoriety as a musician, and was busy playing with several little bands that found plenty of work in the Sioux Falls area. He often took me, a mischievous roustabout five-year-old, with him to his Sioux Falls gigs.

It was a thrill to go along and to listen to the music, watch the band perform, and see the people dancing and enjoying themselves. Dad was on stage most of the time, of course, so he'd find an empty chair for me, sit me down and tell me not to wander far from it. Ordinarily, bedtime for me was 9 p.m. or so. But on these special "boys' night out" sessions with Dad, we'd be up half the night. I'm sure I drifted away from my assigned chair from time to time, but most of the time I was listening to the music and watching those happy people dancing and enjoying the evening.

Sometimes, Dad would call me up on stage and set me down behind the drum set. I'd never had lessons, but the beat seemed to come naturally to me. I'd bang away, stretching far to make sure my foot was on the bass drum pedal just right so that I could still reach the snares and the cymbals. I particularly remember that my little impromptu gig with the band would include a rousing rendition of "Do Doly Do." And I also remember helping the band with a song called "Whispering."

Drumming with the band was great fun for me. But I also enjoyed the applause. I liked it and the thrill emerged again in my high school years to help in my decision to become a professional musician. I wanted to be just like my dad and his musical avocation.

I have nothing but fond memories of my childhood and of my adventures as a youngster growing up in Sioux Falls. I can remember as far back as about 1945 when I was four. We were poor, but I didn't know that we were. I didn't think we were any different than anyone else, and perhaps that is the beauty of youth. We are all equal in the eyes of the young.

There was an old upright piano in our dining room, its veneer in some places yearning to be free and several of the ivory keys that had already had their wish for freedom answered. But despite its worn look, it was a beautiful thing to me. It had a bench with a hinged lid, and inside was a jumble of sheet music that was seldom, if ever, used. Dad played the piano by ear and that's how I learned to do it, too. Although I was only five, I was fascinated with that old upright. If he was there playing it, I was there on his lap, watching his every move. We had several songs we both liked, and one I remember was "Darktown Strutters Ball." By the time I was six he'd taught me how to play chords. For reasons now unknown, most of the songs he taught me were played on the black keys, in "F"sharp and a few in the key of "C."

Later, when I was attending Lincoln Grade School, I found the school piano back in the corner of the gymnasium. I would play it whenever I got a chance, such as when rain or winter weather was not conducive to recess. I'd hike myself up on the piano bench, sit on my knees and play songs by ear as Dad did. Students and teachers gathered round to listen and made requests. Although I was shy, I admit that I enjoyed the attention and being in the limelight and at times it made me feel special.

Except for what my dad showed me, I've never had a piano lesson. I've always played my music by ear. Even in grade school, if I heard a song once, I could sit down and nine times out of ten play it right through. I pictured in my mind what keys and what notes I needed to touch as if I had a little keyboard packed away in some crevice of my cranium somewhere. I could look at the keys and in my mind I knew exactly what they sounded like. Even today, I still see that little piano when I hear a song. It's weird in a way. Once, my mother invested some of her hard-earned money to pay for accordion lessons for me. It was a waste. I had difficulty reading the notes and found it all very boring.

One of my aunts, Myra Wachendorf, was a wonderful teacher, but lacked natural ability at the piano. She taught music for many years in the Marion-Parker area and was well known for her talent to teach. But in my mind, people like Aunt Myra who aren't born with natural talent and therefore play by only reading the music, sound too mechanical. I've always felt, and I've learned from observation, that most of the great musicians are the ones who have a natural talent and a flair for showmanship, plus know how to read music so they have the whole package. Two examples are Liberace, the gaudily-dressed piano player, and that great accordion player from South Dakota, Myron Floren.

By the end of the nation's roller coaster ride through the 1940s, my dad had established himself as a top salesman at Weatherwax. Servicemen were returning with money saved, and needed civilian clothes. Dad was a gregarious, friendly guy with a good memory for names, and he had many repeat customers. Many took the time to drive up from his hometown of Marion, and from around the Parker area, too. If he was busy with another customer, they waited for him.

Each August, it was our family's custom to go to the Turner County Fair in Parker. The fair was a big attraction, one of *the* biggest in the state. The grounds were always packed with people. Most of them, I remember, knew my parents. We did the usual fair things, with mom assigned the responsibility of herding us around, of riding with us on the Ferris wheel, the tilt-a-whirl and the merry-go-round and filling us up with cotton candy and hot dogs.

Dad, meanwhile, made the rounds, visiting with old friends. He would combine business with pleasure. Dad had a knack for relating to the public, which perhaps came from the hundreds of hours he'd spent in his life up on stage and entertaining the crowds. For the Turner County Fair, he always took along an ample supply of yellow work gloves then popular with farmers. Like a politician trolling for votes, Dad handed out his business card with his picture on it to every farmer he met, and sweetened the pie with a pair of those brand new gloves. He did well at Weatherwax's because of the clientele he developed with this and other goodwill gestures. I remember once he showed mom his commission check. It came to over $600 for just one month. That was a fortune in my mind back then, and it was also a big pocket full to any adult in 1949, too.

With the economic times continuing to improve after the war ended, people were using any surplus cash they earned to buy the extras of the good life that the Depression, and the war that followed, had denied them. Dad used some of his commission money to buy a new car. He drove home one day with a sparkling new, creamy white 1949 Chevrolet Styleline Special. It cost him $1,700. He paid extra for a cigarette lighter in the dash, but declined to have a clock installed because of its cost. His wristwatch would tell him all he needed to know about time, he said. And he told the dealer not to install a radio, either, which also cost extra. The new Chevy was, however, all decked out in the gaudy chrome that seemed to hold cars together in those early post-war years. The car was his pride and joy, his first new car ever. By the time I was nineteen, I was buying new cars that cost several times more than what my dad had managed to scrape together for his.

One summer we drove in that new car to the Black Hills. For us, it was a very big deal, especially crossing over the roiling-wide Missouri at Chamberlain, and staring down the glass-caged snakes at Reptile Gardens up on Rockerville Hill south of Rapid City. Of course, we didn't have a radio to help pass the traveling time as we hummed along across the state at 55 mph. But we all sang loudly to make up for that.

Probably as a carry-over from the practice by motorists of the 1930s and the early 1940s when the old cars of the day overheated easily, Dad, who was a Cub Scout troop leader and therefore was always prepared, packed a couple gallons of water in the trunk for our trip across the state, even though we were in a brand new car. Fortunately, the radiator never called out for more water.

Consumer goods were becoming more accessible to everyone by 1949. Not just new cars for dads, but new toys for kids who until then had to make do with worn-out brooms, hand-me-down toys in various states of disrepair, sling shots made of tree branches, or whatever they could find to play with. My most memorable Christmas gift ever was in 1949 when I unwrapped a classy Lionel electric train set.

I also remember that during that Christmas Eve in 1949, Dad had a very bad cold and a fever. He remained in bed while we kids and Mom opened our presents.

We didn't know it at the time, but his illness was a harbinger of sad times that were bearing down upon our little family.

I didn't think much of his illness at the time. He didn't seem to get any better. By New Year's Day he was still bedridden. His health continued to deteriorate. By February 1950, Dr. Howard Shreves recommended to Mom that she take him to Sioux Valley Hospital. It must have been a serious illness, but of course, we three Wachendorf kids had no idea just how serious. During succeeding days, Dad's condition worsened. I was eight years old at the time, but I remember the concern in my mother's face and the worry in her quivering voice. Dad now had developed an infection in his kidneys and there were, at that time, few treatments or antibiotics. I later learned that he was suffering with Brights disease.

The day he died began like every other day for us kids. We were up early, downed a hurried oatmeal breakfast, and then were off to Lincoln Elementary School across the street, except for brother Marv, who was just three years old. That afternoon, when we got home from school, Mom asked a neighbor to come over to stay with Marv while my sister Marlene, Mom and I went to the hospital. Mom talked with Dad for a while and then we had to leave for supper. Before we left I edged over and stood by my dad's hospital bed. He reached out and took my hand. I can still hear his voice even now, soft and halting. "Go with Mom now," he said, looking into my eyes. "And you always remember to be a good boy and to mind your mother." Those were the last words he ever said to me. During my life I have tried to live up to what he told me so many years ago.

About an hour after we got home from the hospital, the telephone rang. Mom answered and then she started to cry. Dad wouldn't be coming home, she told us. He had died. Later that evening, Dad's three brothers and their wives came to our house and I remember that before we kids were sent to bed, they were all sitting around our kitchen table. The brothers were crying and it gave me, an eight-year-old, a strange feeling. I'd never seen grown men cry. The women later moved into the living room and talked and we three kids were allowed to stay up for a while beyond our normal bedtime. When Mom told us it was time for bed, we traipsed up the stairs to our room. As we did, I could hear my Aunt Edna in the living room say to Mom: "I just can't believe Robert is dead—such a young man—he was only 33 years old." I will never forget what she said. My dad seemed old to me, and 33 seemed so very old in my mind. I hadn't thought of him as young. But he was.

Later, as I stood with Mom, Marlene, and little brother Marv in the gray, nearly colorless day at the cemetery in Marion, west of Sioux Falls, I wondered what changes were in store for our family with Dad gone.

2

The Family Survives

Of course, there were many changes awaiting the four-member Bob Wachendorf family. He had been the breadwinner. Now, our already limited family budget had to be pared even more. The first thing that Mom did was move into a small apartment near the larger home at 947 West Eighth that we had been renting.

To help until our lives returned to something more normal, my Aunt Edna and Uncle Waggie offered to take me in with them. They lived about three blocks from us, so I was still close to my grade school. Mom reluctantly agreed to send me there for a few months. Waggie, whose real name was Bill, was an automobile parts man for more than thirty years at the local Buick garage and dealership, then located across from the bus depot on Seventh Street.

At first it seemed a welcome adventure for me to spend time with Uncle Waggie. For one, he played the mandolin. And sometimes his son, my cousin Mory, joined in, playing a wonderful black comb covered with some tissue paper. We often teamed up, with me on the piano. Our impromptu concerts always included Uncle Waggie's favorite "Turkey In The Straw." I had only been there a few days when homesickness settled in. Aunt Edna must have noticed my unhappiness, because within a week I was back home. Although I loved my Uncle Waggie and Aunt Edna, I was very glad to be back with my immediate family.

Friends and relatives of my parents were supportive and more than helpful during those very difficult first few months after Dad's death. A neighbor, kindly Mrs. Moi, dropped by to visit us every evening for many, many weeks. Often, she came carrying a steaming casserole wrapped in a dish towel, or brought over a cake or a pie for a snack. She had eight children at home to care for and her husband was bedridden. But bless her heart, she seemed to always save a little of her considerable care and concern for us.

Preparing for a friendly game of Canasta at the Wachendorf home are from left, Marlene Wachendorf, Mrs. Moi, standing, Alice Wachendorf, seated, and Myron. Mrs. Moi, a neighbor, was a welcomed friend and cheerful visitor during the days following the death of Bob Wachendorf when Myron was eight.

A few weeks after Dad died, Mom began to look for work. Never in her life had she worked outside the home, so the ordeal must have been difficult. She finally found work at Fantle's Department Store, and since we lived near a bus stop, she took the bus to work each morning. She earned $40 working six days a week. For that first Christmas without Dad in 1950, prospects for gifts for us seemed slim. But our guardian angel, Mrs. Moi, was there for us once again. She brought over gifts for all three of us kids and for Mom. And what gifts they were. Mine was something that, aside from the Lionel train set that Dad bought for me the previous year, I'll always remember. It was a balloon-tired Schwinn bike. It was used, but I didn't know, and I didn't really care. It was a bike! Mrs. Moi later told me she got it from a bike repairman in town known as Fred the Fixer. It still had the swooping, streamlined tank between the cross bars, multi-colored plastic streamers attached to the ends of the handlebars, and a working headlight swiveling around on the handlebars. A nine-year-old kid on a balloon-tired bike with plastic streamers and a headlight to boot can push off and bravely explore a whole new neighborhood. Even if it was December and January, it wasn't long before I knew every sidewalk bike-hazard for blocks around our house.

That 1950 Christmas Eve was also memorable for another reason. We'd finished our evening meal when Mr. Frank Weatherwax, for whom my Dad had worked, dropped by. He wished us all a Merry Christmas and before he left he handed my mother an envelope. She cried when she opened it and found a crisp $100 bill inside. For many Christmases thereafter, Mr. Weatherwax would drop by on Christmas Eve with an envelope and the welcome gift of cash. He was a caring, kindly gentleman who helped make Christmas a little more joyful for Mrs. Wachendorf and her kids, and I will always remember his thoughtfulness.

We were still living near Lincoln Grade School and also a short bike ride away from Doring's Grocery Store. It was common for a bunch of us kids to scramble into the store after school, all intent on getting a penny's worth of candy or a bottle of soda pop, except for me. Doring's Store had a long, white, look-in meat counter common then. It occupied one side of the store, and in it among the steaks

Myron, 10, in his Cub Scout uniform. His dad, Bob, was den leader.

and mounds of red hamburger and pork chops was what I considered to be a flat-out delicacy. Rather than buy pop or candy, I invested in cold wieners. Mr. Doring charged me three cents for each one. I still enjoy an uncooked hot dog now and then, but the going rate today is probably more than three cents apiece.

Other neighborhood sights and delights that I remember arrived by horse cart. There was the Lakeside Dairy wagon packed with milk, butter, and cream. In the summer, there was the ice wagon that produced slivers of ice for the kids whenever blocks were sized and weighed for the neighborhood iceboxes. Those with iceboxes in need of ice would place a twelve-inch square sign in their front window as a signal to the iceman.

Another exciting summer treat was the day the circus came to town. We rode our bikes down to the train station to watch the unloading amidst the shouts and barks of the circus crews, punctuated with the snorts, brays, and grunts of the animals happy to be earthbound again after a long train ride. The procession of animals and equipment in the circus wagons would head down Eighth Street past our house on the way to the Fairgrounds. We tagged along in its wake, and then watched the men set up the huge tents, helped along by dutiful elephants who seemed to know the procedure as well as the men. I later found a strange similarity between the helter-skelter, noisy, somewhat confusing circus preparations with the stage setup our band went through before each appearance.

There was never a lull or loss for ways to spend those glorious summer days in Sioux Falls. There were long swims at the Terrace Park Pool. After summer rains, armed with a flashlight, there were forays into the dark, hunting gigantic night crawlers that I kept in a big washtub filled with dirt out in the garage. The worms were worth from twenty-five to thirty cents a dozen. I advertised on a sign I made and stuck out in the front yard. One night the hunting was particularly good. I personally captured over 1,200 crawlers, and packaged them into 100 containers, a dozen in each. I soon "grew" my night crawler business to include resorts near

Sioux Falls. The owners came in to buy all I could provide. One summer, I made $100, and I thought I was very rich. I guess that I was.

In about 1952, with Mom working at Fantle's and a small amount of government aid for us kids, we were able to move to a larger house at 211 North Prairie a few blocks from where we had been living. For some reason, we didn't take our old upright piano with us in that move.

Everyone was very kind to our family. Since we no longer had our faithful old piano, and I enjoyed playing piano very much, I often went over to Mr. and Mrs. Paul Alvine's house next door, and played an upright they had in their basement. One day, it magically appeared in our living room. Recently, I visited with Dr. Frank Alvine, now a respected and well-known orthopedic surgeon in Sioux Falls, and he told me the story of how the Alvine piano ended up at our house. It had been used by Dr. Frank Alvine's sister, and now, young Frank was expected to take lessons, practice on that piano in their basement, and become proficient at it.

Myron Wachendorf in 1954 enjoying time on the piano in his home. The piano was a gift of the Paul Alvine family, who lived next door. Mrs. Alvine knew of Myron's love of piano because he was always at the Alvine's house playing it. So one day she had it moved over to the Wachendorf house.

But like most boys, the future surgeon had other adventures and explorations in mind. So Mrs. Alvine, knowing of my interest in playing the piano after I'd spent many hours banging away at it in the basement, had the piano moved over to our house. Dr. Frank said that the first inclination he had that his piano playing days were over was one day after school, when he went down in the basement for his practice session, and discovered the piano was gone. He said he complained very little when he learned of the gift to the Wachendorf family. I was thrilled to have it and have always appreciated what Mrs. Alvine did.

Our new home and new piano at 211 North Prairie Avenue were just three houses down from the Augustana Lutheran Church. Being so close, Mom insisted we attend Sunday School on a regular basis. On many Sundays after church, Mom would back Dad's 1949 Chevy out of the garage and we'd drive to Parker to visit my maternal grandmother, Grandma Mary Dice, or to visit at Claude and Louise's farm. Grandma Mary was from Russia and she and others settled in the Parker area in 1912. She lived in a tiny house on the edge of town. I remember that when we arrived, she would be listening to religious music on her radio, the songs beaming out over WNAX in Yankton. She also loved country-western music, as I did, and she would often send away for autographed pictures of stars like Gene Autry, Hopalong Cassidy, and my favorite, Roy Rogers and Trigger, to give to me. Once, when Dad was still alive, he took me to the Coliseum to see Gene Autry and his horse Champion on stage there.

My friend and schoolmate, Roger Dearduff, lived next door to the south of us. Mr. Paul Alvine had a recorder and he often made recordings of me playing. Roger would provide moral support during these impromptu sessions. Mr. Alvine's recorder used a vinyl disk. I'd play the piano and, with Roger as his assistant, he served as the sound engineer and recorded my music. My faithful playmate Roger, incidentally, later became a successful Chevrolet car dealer in Dell Rapids. But those early recording sessions with Roger and Dr. Alvine were, I believe, when I started to think that one day perhaps I could be a famous piano player. But then it was just a dream. I had no idea how to go about it.

At home, along with our new piano, we also had an old RCA phonograph with a crank to a power spring. It played 78 rpm records. Whenever the money I earned from my two paper routes, my Christmas card door-to-door sales, or my night crawler sales allowed, I invested in records. I had a big collection of all the songs and music by the big bands and popular singers of the day and listened to them endlessly. I nearly wore out my shoulders lugging the big bags containing thick Sunday *Minneapolis Tribune* newspapers, and every Thursday I also delivered the *Sioux Falls Shopping News* after school. Once, the *Minneapolis Tribune* sponsored a subscription drive contest for paperboys and girls. I knocked on all the doors in the neighborhood and twice won trips to the Twin Cities. I got to see George Miken play basketball with the Minneapolis Lakers. I also won a new bike to replace the old Schwinn from Mrs. Moi that had now been relegated to that great bike rack in the sky.

In the early 1950s, I set my record collecting habit aside long enough to buy our family a television set. Of course, I also had a selfish reason for buying it, too. It was a nineteen-inch Admiral, black and white, because in those days color television seemed a dream. After I brought it home, Mom took a picture of me standing beside it and sent her snapshot in to the Minneapolis paper. The *Tribune* printed it as an example of the possibilities for potential earnings for paper carriers.

I got the TV set from Bob Niblick, owner of Sioux Falls Music. I'd had my eye on the set in the store display window for months. It had a price tag of $199, or about two seasons of my night crawler business. I was eleven at the time and the magic brought into living rooms by television was a big attraction for me. I especially enjoyed the musical shows. I also watched Verne Gagne and the professional wrestling shows, and just knew the fighting was for real, when it actually wasn't. I also found the Gillette Friday Night Fights of great interest. Those were for real.

In 1953, two years after his father died, Myron saved $199 and bought his family a nineteen-inch, black and white Admiral television set at Sioux Falls Music. He made monthly payments until the bill was paid.

My television interest was piqued while visiting at my good friend Steven Zick's house. They had a set and he often invited me over to the house to watch. One night in May 1953, we watched KELO-TV sign on for the first time ever. The station aired the historic test pattern from 6 p.m. to 7 p.m. when the first program came on. It was *Dragnet*, with Badge #714 Joe Friday. Incidentally, I'm told that Dave Deadrick, a.k.a. Captain 11, was the first local voice to be heard over the new station. Days before the first program, Steven and I sat around red-eyed, hypnotized by the squiggly test pattern that by some miracle appeared on the Zick family screen.

I was hooked. I told Bob down at the music store that I was interested in the set in the window, but admitted that I only had $100 saved up. We agreed that I could pay the rest at $10 a month. We shook hands and sealed the deal. In ten months I had the set paid off. An unintended consequence of the inauguration of television in Sioux Falls, and in every town, was the eventual loss of the theaters. In Sioux Falls, the count went from seven theaters to just two downtown, but there was a welcome rebound years later when the malls were built.

Each summer during my growing up years I spent several weeks at my Aunt Louise and Uncle Claude Bovee's farm near Parker. Their son Arnold and his wife Fern farmed nearby, so I alternated between both places. It was an enjoyable and educational time for me, and I came to love life on the farm. Once, when a cow was having birthing difficulties, Uncle Claude invited me along to the barn to assist him in the birth. The calf's hind legs were out, so Uncle Claude and I pulled as the mother bellowed and moaned. Eventually the newborn calf emerged. Frankly, until then, I hadn't been certain where those cute little calves gallivanting around the farm had actually came from.

Summer storms on the prairies of South Dakota are common and it seemed they always timed their arrival around Parker to my stay at the Bovee farm. As the heavy clouds rolled in, Aunt Louise herded us down into the dank, dark fruit cellar—a small, dugout cave where the canned fruits and vegetables were kept and the sauerkraut bubbled in a big crock covered with a board held in place with a hefty field stone. She'd light a candle down there in the dark, and we'd stay close to her, mindful of the critters, real and imaginary, that young minds assume would find welcome solace in such a cool, depressing place that smelled like dirt.

Every day we were all up before dawn to gather eggs and care for the animals and then milk eight or ten cows eagerly waiting for us each morning. Uncle Claude let me help with the milking, and I thought I was making a contribution to the chores. Looking back now, I was probably in his way more than I was being a productive assistant. But I thought I was helping. Cats familiar with the routine occupied strategic stations nearby as we harvested milk. For sport, Uncle Claude would give them a well-placed squirt from time to time, which amused me greatly. I'd even chase a stream of milk headed in my general direction, and occasionally get a gulp of it plus spillage on my face, which greatly amused Uncle Claude, and maybe even the cats.

During the day, fortified with a big breakfast, I went with Uncle Claude and his son Arnold to the fields. It was a favorite part of the workday. With my uncle riding shotgun and watching over me, I drove the tractor to the work site. Arnold followed in a 1936 Chevy that the chickens loved to decorate in black and white. Because that car was probably safer for a nine-year-old than the tractor, I got to drive that old 1936 Chevy solo back to the farmhouse to get the traditional afternoon lunch at about 3:30 p.m. each day. Once out of sight of Uncle Claude, I would wrap the old straight stick machine and spin the wheels, or just go a little faster than Uncle Claude would have approved. I'd pick up the sandwiches and Kool-Aid and head back to the field for what to me was a regular picnic in the tractor shade. If it was a busy time, we'd work in the field until early evening, so the afternoon lunch was a welcome carryover for the long days.

My other responsibility was driving the Chevy out to the mailbox along the main road to pick up the mail. The township road was a mile away. With my farm-tanned left arm resting on the doorsill the way my dad used to drive, my trip to the mailbox seemed to me like another trip to Rapid City in Dad's old 1949 Styleline.

I think I would have been a good farmer just like Claude and Arnold, except I only liked to do the fun stuff. I hated the rainy days when I fussed around in the sheds while machinery was repaired and serviced. Fixing fences and cutting cockleburs were not my favorite chores, either. But I enjoyed the routine and the camaraderie with Claude and Arnold. By the time I was ten I was steering a Ford tractor down the rows cultivating corn and helping load hay bales.

Saturday night was the best part of farm life. We quit work early on Saturday, had a sponge bath because running water wasn't available, and primped and primed for the trip to town. Claude had a brand new 1953 Chevy that had its week's collection of garage dust removed for the six-mile trip to Parker. The countryside emptied as every man, woman and child, plus some of the better behaved dogs in the area, headed to town. There, the farm families sold their eggs and cream and maybe some chickens. They stocked up on supplies for the next week and they caught up on all of the community news and gossip.

Parker's wide main street would be wall-to-wall people and curb-to-curb cars, with another platoon of them lined haphazardly down the middle of the street. There was that wonderful carnival atmosphere and the aroma of fried onions and hamburger mingled with cigar smoke and the smell of popcorn bouncing around in the glass case at the little stand on the corner. The place was filled with the hum of commerce and the buzz of chit-chat as happy people in that farming community came together.

Some Saturdays we'd take in a movie, but most of the time it was a continuous stroll up and down the street seeing people who knew my uncle and who had known my dad. It was a compliment for me to hear people say I looked "just like Bob." Uncle Claude would also take me into the pool hall where he played cards or eight ball at the pool table. As I waited and tried to act much older than I was, he'd let me sip a cold glass of beer. I was just ten, but he let me drink away. It had a bitter and different taste, but I enjoyed it. Perhaps that's part of my German heritage. Uncle Claude did set a limit of just one small glass for me just once a week.

The evening ended about 10 p.m. Townspeople hung around to watch the exodus—especially the jostling of the cars as they untangled from unfamiliar traffic jams. Sunday mornings we were at the Lutheran Church. Sunday afternoons were times of rest and visiting day on the farm. Relatives came to enjoy the company and Aunt Louise's scrumptious dinner, which she topped off later with homemade pie, cake and ice cream, or fresh strawberries from the garden. Then it was Sunday afternoon siesta time.

Both Claude and Arnold had pianos in their homes and both played by ear. Apparently, music and entertainment runs in the Wachendorf and Bovee families. Like my dad, they, too, had been part of the little bands that played dances and socials in the area. I learned a lot from watching them.

Those wonderful summers near Parker didn't end until I enrolled in Washington High School in the fall of 1956. When it was time for me to go back home to Mom, there was one final stop at the clothing store in Parker. Claude and Louise bought new clothes and school supplies for me. How generous and thoughtful that was. Both the men, who were like fathers to me, are gone now. Claude died at the ripe age of 101 and Arnold passed away at age 72. Aunt Louise is still with us and is a joy at 97. Fern is also still part of our extended family. I've told them many times how important those years were to me and how they all meant so much in my life. Incidentally, after my other responsibilities ended my summers at Parker, my younger brother Marv took over. His memories are the same, including the final late summer stop in Parker for new clothes and school items, compliments of Louise and Claude.

During my high school years after the summers on the farm, I discovered a new kind of music and found that music, not farming, would be my niche in life.

3

A New Sound in Popular Music

In the early 1950s, when I was ten or eleven, Saturday afternoon movies were an escape from girls and reality, and it became one of my favorite pastimes. My buddies and I usually took in a cowboy movie at the Granada at Eighth and Phillips, digging out a dime from among the jackknife and Double Bubble gum package in a deep blue jean pocket, and getting a ticket and a penny back. I was an avid western movie fan. When I was younger I was the proud owner of an authentic Roy Rogers cowboy outfit complete with spurs and a dandy pearl-handled pistol encased in a Roy Rogers holster that glistened with inserted red rubies or diamonds or something just as valuable, in my eyes, at least. Also in my arsenal was a Daisy BB gun for added protection out on the range.

I consumed Roy Rogers comic books by the dozens and traded them with fellow fans of Roy and Trigger. I listened to Skyking on the radio and Bobby Benson and the B-Bar-B Riders. I defended Roy's honor with other buddies, who preferred Gene Autry or Hopalong Cassidy, or some other cowhand of movie fame. Once, I sent in a Quaker Oats cereal box coupon and a dime for a Roy Rogers ring that I proudly wore until it turned green. It had a secret compartment for secret notes. Growing up, I must have ridden a thousand miles with old Roy, and with secret notes hidden away, during my imaginary séances.

Later in life, my wife Carole and I had the opportunity to meet Roy Rogers in person when we toured his museum in Victorville, CA. That was about six years before he died on July 6, 1998. Roy was about eighty years old when we met him. When we walked into the museum and saw Roy Rogers standing there before us, it was dream come true for me. He still looked fit and trim, but of course, he was no longer the vibrant King of the Cowboys defending justice, arresting rustlers,

As a youngster, Roy Rogers was Myron's favorite movie cowboy. Much later, when he and his wife Carole, and brother-in-law Larry Wesendorf, vacationed in California, they toured the Roy Rogers Museum in Victorville, where they met the aging star. That was two years before his death. Roy was on a golf cart because he had grown weary of walking.

and singing "Tumbling Tumbleweeds." We toured the museum early in the morning before the crowds began to arrive. So when we saw Roy we stopped to talk to him. He was friendly and outgoing. He remembered pheasant hunts he'd had in South Dakota in earlier years. We stopped to talk near a large glass case that held the stuffed carcass of his Palomino horse Trigger. I asked Roy about the horse and he said he still thought of Trigger almost every day. He mentioned that he still lived on a ranch outside of town, but later when I visited with his daughter she said he had a condo on the golf course. She explained to me that he told visitors he still lived on a ranch because he felt that's where they expected him to be living. Meeting Roy Rogers on that vacation was the highlight of the trip. In fact, I would have driven to California just to meet him.

Back in Sioux Falls in the early 1950s, when not attending Roy Rogers movies, we explored downtown Sioux Falls and the big department stores there before the era of mile-long malls. We especially liked the J. C. Penney Store and the rides on the escalator until an officious clerk or the manager began to look at us questionably.

Another fond memory was the culinary treat available at the Coney Island that was located next to the Granada Theater. The place served the world's best chili dog. An elderly Greek man owned the place and had devised his own secret recipe for the chili. The story is that when he died, the recipe for that delicious treat went with him. If I could turn back the clock and stroll around in downtown Sioux Falls, one of my first stops would be to buy a guitar case full of those wonderful chili dogs. In the 1960s, before the owner died, my neighbor and good friend Bob Brownell and I would buy sacks full to take home to eat while his girlfriend and my wife Carole watched television. Those dogs had staying power. On the way home, the grease would seep through the sack and settle in on the car seat upholstery. That was okay because then I could enjoy that wonderful aroma for days afterwards.

If we were hungry for a double egg burger, we'd drift two blocks south to Tenth Street and the Hamburger Inn owned for many years by Stan and Aubry, who were there day and night cooking those twenty-cent burgers in grease by the front window. When they turned the patties with a well-worn spatula, the grease would spatter up onto the window that was rarely cleaned. The Hamburger Inn burgers had an aroma all their own that you could sniff out from blocks away if the wind was just right.

Dessert was nearby, across the street at Fenns. A small box of damaged Walnut Crush candy bars was sold there for just fifty cents because the packages contained pieces of the bars that had been broken in the manufacturing process.

By 1955, when I was fourteen, I was an awkward, 130-pound freshman wandering anxious and unsure through the hallowed halls of Washington High School. If a girl spoke to me, or even so much as looked my way, I tended to turn beet red, look at my shoes, and wish for powers possessed by the Invisible Man of comic book fame. And my tastes in music changed that year. With my best friend Chuck Molter, we attended the movie at the Hollywood Theater called *Blackboard Jungle*. That movie's theme song, "Rock Around The Clock," was arguably one of the most influential single records to come along in the last half of the twentieth century. I know it changed my life and marked an historic change in music as we had all known it up to that time.

Bill Haley and the Comets worked out of Chester, PA. There had been other rock and roll songs before July 1955, some by Bill Haley and later by others, including The King, Elvis Presley. But it was the hammering beat of "Rock Around The Clock" that firmly established rock and roll in the public's psyche. It had a one-two punch to it that got your attention. The song proved that rock and roll was far from a momentary fad. No less than Paul McCartney and John Lennon later acknowledged the influence of Bill Haley and "Rock Around The Clock." After that movie, Chuck and I, and everyone, were listening to Little Richard, Gene Vincent, and Fats Domino, among others. And, of course, let's not forget that young swivel-hipped man out of Humes High School in Memphis, TN, who rode in on the rock and roll wave, too. "Mystery Train" and "That's Alright Mama" on the Sun record label, were the first Elvis songs that I can remember hearing.

I was enthralled by the rock and roll music pounding out from the theater speakers at the Hollywood Theater that day. What I heard would have a profound effect on my life. Some kids were out of their seats, dancing in the aisle.

By the time I was a freshman at Washington High School, the beckoning beat of rock and roll music was taking over. I had finally saved enough to buy a decrepit old 1947 Chevy. Its tinny-sounding radio was always tuned to the station that was playing music. I think I drove the oldest and least expensive car ($85) of any in my freshman class, which incidentally, included a fellow named George S. Mickelson, who later became governor of the state. I quit school before graduating because of the demands on my music career. So while George was our state's chief executive he gave me an honorary Washington High School graduation diploma. It was presented to me at our class reunion during "Myron Lee Day in South Dakota," which he had decreed.

I now also had a janitor's job after school at the Fashion City ladies store. Because of all of my part-time job commitments, I didn't have time in school to participate in sports, band, or chorus, but I never regretted it. I knew that it was strictly up to me to earn the money I needed for those things I felt were important in my life—like a car and records and, of course, by now, girls. I began to take a shine to a girl who lived across the street from me named Karen Schanck. I would often meet her at school dances and events, but I still lacked the social graces and the nerve to ask her for a date to a movie or a Teen Hop.

Even today, when I hear "Rock Around The Clock" I'm back at the movie in the Hollywood Theater and I see again the look on my friend Chuck's face when the movie started. I've always been amazed that music can transport us back in time. Buddy Holly's song "Maybe Baby," does that for me, too. I'm 17, driving my 1949 Ford, painted in the then very stylish if not pretty gray primer paint, tooling along West Twelfth Street in Sioux Falls near Bob's Drive-In. Buddy's guitar player is perfect, and the Crickets are chiming in and chills run down my spine. It's like that smell of new mown alfalfa when you're out driving a South Dakota country road. The aroma brings back memories of the wonderful summers I spent on my uncles' farms near Parker.

"Rock Around the Clock," and the other tunes and the television programs of the 1950s remain fresh in my mind, and they all were an influence on me. I remember watching *Coke Time with Eddie Fisher* and his song "Oh My Papa," or "Anytime." No Saturday back then was complete without watching the cigarette-sponsored *Lucky Strike Hit Parade*. It featured the week's biggest hits and we all waited to learn what they would be, and if our favorite remained in first place. I remember the Lucky Strike Singers and Dancers and the wonderfully talented soloists like Snooky Lanson, Eileen Wilson, Dorothy Collins, and Gisele McKenzie. Incidentally, I always thought Snooky should have changed his name to something more sophisticated to enhance his image.

I think of the music of that era and I remember the sad lament "Cry" that Johnnie Ray sang with such feeling that he actually shed tears as he sang it. He also made "The Little White Cloud That Cried" and was able to bring tears to his eyes with that one, too. The enthusiastic McGuire Sisters were among my favorites until I learned they hung out with the Mafia big guys in Las Vegas. I also remember Tennessee Ernie Ford's "Sixteen Tons" and everyone singing along.

Many of my friends had boxy, little RCA Victor record players in their rooms at home. The large 78 rpm records in my collection were no longer in vogue. The new craze were the small vinyl 45 rpm records that looked like oversized donuts with the big hole in the middle. They became the popular conveyors of popular music.

By now I not only had my two paper routes, but I was working evenings at Bob Sommer's Grange Avenue Drug Store as a janitor and stock boy. The store closed at 10 p.m. so I would walk down at about 8:30 and began sweeping the floor, emptying the wastebaskets, and stocking the shelves. Friday nights were reserved for mopping the floor. Bob was a wonderful man to work for and he paid me well. I earned fifty cents an hour plus I had what I considered at the time the best fringe benefit ever devised by humankind. Bob gave me free access to anything at the soda fountain. I would purposely delay visiting the fountain while I worked because of the reward I had in mind for myself when I was finished. My favorite was a large root beer float in a mug big as a fruit jar and frosty as a windowpane on a cold winter's morning.

I wasn't old enough at that time to drive a car without a special permit, but with the money I earned I bought a used Cushman motor scooter for $85. Chuck Molter also had a Cushman, so we'd convoy around town proud as punch with our new, "powerful" machines. The one problem with those little scooters was that the engines were air cooled, and if they got too hot, they stopped working, so we often had to sit around on the curb somewhere in Sioux Falls and wait for the engines to cool down.

I also had enough money from the drug store work and my paper routes to continue my habit of stocking up on records at ninety-nine cents each from either Sioux Falls Music Store or Odlands Music Store. I spent many long hours in my room listening to my latest acquisitions and digging out old ones from my collection. I knew by heart most of the words, and would sing along. I always thought I could be a big winner on the television show *Name That Tune*. My memory for lyrics would prove valuable later when, out on the road, I had about two hundred different songs filed away in my head for immediate recall.

Myron with his Cushman Motor Scooter in 1953. He bought it used for $85, using money he earned from his various jobs.

By 1957, when I was a high school sophomore, I took my first halting steps toward a career in music. I started a little combo composed of three of us Washington High School students. I played piano and Greg Hall was the drummer. We also had a string bass player. We practiced after school when we had time and

Singer Gene Vincent at the Arkota Ballroom in Sioux Falls in 1958. At the time he had a top hit on Capitol Records, "Be Bop A Lula." After his performance, a young Myron Wachendorf, aka Myron Lee, at right, waited on stage to get Vincent's autograph.

we started to sound pretty good. The only television station in town then was KELO. It had a locally produced half hour Saturday morning program called *Tomorrow's Stars*. It featured mainly singers, dancers, and musicians from Sioux Falls and the area.

I wrote to the host of the show, Gwen Gustad, and asked if she might consider asking us to come on as guests. Much to my surprise, she said yes. We showed up and played a couple of songs. Apparently we passed the test, because a few weeks later she asked us back. Then Gwen asked if we might become the house band to back up singers who didn't have a band with them. Was she kidding? We were thrilled to do it and spent the rest of our sophomore year on television every Saturday. It was a great opportunity and a thrilling compliment, especially so when the kids at school would stop us in the hall and tell us they had seen us on television.

By 1958, rock and roll music was sweeping the nation. It was, in the vernacular of the day, hot stuff. The impetus that finally pushed me into the music business happened at a Thursday night Teen Hop at the Arkota Ballroom. Country singer Sonny James was the star of the Hop. He had a huge crossover hit called "Young Love." I stood in front of the stage with several hundred other kids that night, enthralled with James' music. I told myself then and there at the Arkota that what Sonny James was doing was what I wanted to do with my life. If he could do it, I rationalized, so could I.

I decided that if our combo was ever going rise to the top in show business we needed to change our musical style. That would mean I'd no longer be the piano player. I needed to learn the intricacies of an electric guitar. I bought a brand new Harmony and amplifier at Sioux Falls Music for $150. I paid for it by the month because I certainly didn't have that kind of ready cash. The next challenge was to learn to play the thing. A friend, Jerry Haacke, and his sister, Geraldine, often played at their father's tavern on Sixth and Weber called Harold's Tavern. Jerry played pretty good guitar so I asked him to show me the basic cords. A kindly lady named Lil who worked at Fashion City also helped me with the basic guitar cords, and between Jerry and Lil, I soon felt comfortable with my new musical role. Before long I became our group's singer and a rhythm guitar player. I asked another friend, Barry Andrews, to join my group. He played a great saxophone. I added Augustana College student Dick Robinson as drummer, and Jerry Haacke agreed to play lead guitar.

It was a talented group of musicians and it started a tradition of hiring only the best for my band that continued throughout my career. They all made me look good.

With the spots in my band filled, I figured we needed a catchy name. So I decided we'd be The Caddies. Many people always assumed we took the name from the car, but that wasn't the case. I picked that name because some of us sometimes worked as caddies at the Minnehaha County Club. I also thought that it would be a good, clean-cut name that was easy to remember. At that early stage in our careers, we weren't Myron Wachendorf and the Caddies. We were just The Caddies. Another name, easier to say and remember, would come later.

Although I didn't plan it that way and I can't take credit for being clairvoyant, my timing was perfect. There were no other rock and roll bands in the area except a group of Native American boys in the Pierre area that called themselves The Burns Boys, I believe. So in 1958 we got in on the ground floor of South Dakota rock and roll. The ride would last for over thirty-four years.

Our first chance at what I considered the "big time" was at Gene Grebin's Stardust Club on Highway 16 east of town where Washington High School now

The Caddies' first job in 1958 was at Gene Grebin's Startdust Club out on Highway 16 east of Sioux Falls. The attached beer garden is at right. This photo was taken long after the Stardust Club had closed, but before it was torn down.

stands. Gene heard us on the television talent show and called me in the spring of 1958. He asked if we could come out the following Sunday afternoon and play for a couple of hours. The club was small, but had a screened in, attached beer garden with a nice-sized concrete dance floor. We were excited about the opportunity and gladly accepted his offer. All that first week Grebin advertised on the city's top forty radio station KIHO that we would play at the Sunday afternoon event. That Sunday, much to our surprise, The Caddies flat-out packed them in to the place.

Afterwards, Grebin told me that he'd sold a record amount of beer during our two-hour stint—over 200 cases. I can still remember that first live show ever for us. Many of our high school friends came by, and everyone was cheering and clapping and urging us on. Looking back now, I don't think we were that good at that time. But the crowds thought we were tremendous and each person paid a one dollar cover charge to get in. People were actually paying to hear us. I couldn't believe it. And Grebin couldn't wait to hire us back. We ended up playing out there every weekend for the rest of the summer. The place was always filled to capacity, and Grebin gave us each $15 for each performance. He was, of course, making a killing off of our efforts. But we were young and the opportunity was more thrilling than any remuneration he could have provided. We just wanted to perform. Heck, we'd have probably played the Stardust for free.

On some weekends, cars spilled out from the Stardust parking lot and were lined up along the highway as far away as a quarter of a mile from the club each way. Our sound wafted out from The Stardust in great abundance. There was a dairy farm across the street from the club, and the owner complained to Grebin that his cows were giving less milk on Sunday nights because of all the noise they heard Sunday afternoons. We considered that as a compliment.

We picked the music we played at the Stardust by listening during the week to local radio station KIHO playing their Top Forty list. We memorized the words and the music and that way, stayed current on the latest hits. I've never bought a piece

What was once Groveland Park Pavilion near Tyndall is where Myron Lee and the Caddies, while still juniors in high school, played their first out-of-town gig. Today, although still in its original location, it is a machine shed on the Roger and Lori Pietz farm near Tyndall. The round-top part of the structure was originally a dance hall at the Wonderland Park complex east of Yankton. In the 1930s the park became known as Green Gables. In 1939, the building was moved to its present location near Tyndall and became Groveland Park Pavilion.

of sheet music in my life. It would be foreign to me anyway since I can't read music. The Caddies were becoming household names, at least in Sioux Falls and the surrounding area. Radio stations carried Grebin's advertising about us out in a fifty-mile radius.

And as luck would have it, during all of this excitement for the four of us Washington High School juniors, Chuck Molter's father, who had an old-time accordion band, gave us our second opportunity. His group was to play at Groveland Park Ballroom in Tyndall, SD, and Mr. Molter asked me if The Caddies would come down and play during their periodic fifteen-minute intermissions. We took him up on the offer. It was our first out-of-town gig. We rented a U-Haul trailer for our equipment, hitched it up to my 1955 Ford and started out for Tyndall. It was the first trip of what ended up to be thirty-five years and hundreds of thousands of miles traveling to and from jobs.

There was a good crowd at the Groveland Dancehall that Saturday night. Many were young people. During our first fill-in session, the crowd, young and old alike, went absolutely wild. Mr. Molter and his band had been playing the old time music that was still popular with the geriatric crowd. But after we experienced our little fifteen minutes of fame, the crowd booed when the big band stepped back on stage. I felt badly for Mr. Molter and his band members, but I had no control of the situation. Throughout the rest of the evening, the same thing happened. There were cheers for us and boos for the big band when they stepped back on stage after their breaks. That night before we left Groveland Park, the ballroom owner, George Beringer, looked me up and hired us to come back soon.

We were really pumped as we drove the 100 miles back from Tyndall to Sioux Falls in the wee hours of the morning. I decided we needed to get a record out to the radio stations to help our cause. I just knew, after our reception at the Stardust Club in Sioux Falls and the welcome we had received at the Groveland Park

Ballroom, that The Caddies were headed for bigger and better things. I started writing songs and came up with my first two a few weeks after the Tyndall trip.

One was called "Homicide" and the other "Ah, C'mon Baby." "Homicide" was a wacky song about the unpleasant consequences of a drag race between a guy and his girlfriend and an unidentified flying object (UFO). I arranged for The Caddies to have a recording session at the University of South Dakota in Vermillion. We had tapes made that we sent to the HEP record label in St. Paul, MN, a company I had seen advertised in a music magazine.

I ordered 500 records for $400. The company called me the day they sent them out by bus to Sioux Falls. That was a day I'll always remember. We all went down to the bus station and sat in the terminal waiting patiently for the package to arrive. Then we rushed to my home and sat around in my room listening to them over and over again. What a thrill. We sent a copy to several radio stations. At KIHO, the DJ asked listeners to call in to vote on which song they liked the best. "Homicide" won out. The record, incidentally, is now a collector's item and sells for as much as one hundred-fifty dollars. It is especially popular in Europe even today because, they say, it has a unique rock sound.

To help recover my $400 investment in the record, I placed a supply in both Sioux Falls music stores and we also sold them at our dances for a buck each. We didn't make much of a profit, but I recovered my investment. Having a record out, however, was a psychological boost for The Caddies.

Our music business was becoming big business for some rather wide-eyed high school kids who had much to learn. Help in the management of The Caddies was on its way.

4

Help Is on the Way

In 1958, The Caddies were picking up speed and gaining local fame. I thanked my lucky stars, and figured that those heavenly bodies had been aligned just right to influence our successes. Three things happened in the late 1950s that would help chart our future course, too.

One was radio station KIHO and the other two were a couple of great guys who really knew the music business, Bob Helgeson and Jimmy Thomas. Interestingly, both came from Luverne, MN.

All of the folks at KIHO were very kind to us. The station played my new song "Homicide," over and over again. I learned that while word of mouth advertising might make the rock and roll world go around, a friendly radio station sure can't hurt.

In the 1950s, nearly every community of reasonable size had at least two things in common. Each had a farm implement dealership and each had a Top Forty radio station, or picked up a strong signal from a nearby community. Radio was a catalyst for musicians, especially those who were struggling for recognition and a break, as we were. In Sioux Falls, our electronic benefactor was without question Radio KIHO, 1270 on the dial. It was a twenty-four hour, low power station with a big following, especially of young people. The station's cadre of disc jockeys had colorful names to fit their on-air personas. There was Ki-Ho Helgie, Little Phil Severtson, who was actually a fairly large man, Dandy Don, and Smilin' Jack Shaffer. The station was a Pied Piper for the kids, and it played top forty picks from Billboard Magazine's top 100 hits each week.

KIHO also pioneered live remotes in the Sioux Falls area. One of their favorite setups was Earl's Pizza House on Eighth Street. Earl's was the place to be for everybody who was somebody and for others, such as me, who just loved the pizza. Many Sioux Falls old timers still talk about Earl's. It is my opinion, as an amateur pizza aficionado, that no one has yet matched the unique taste of Earl's

27

Myron, just 18, wanted his band to look professional. He found an advertisement in a musician's magazine that offered inexpensive jackets. They came in only three sizes, small, medium, and large. Obviously, the wrong size was ordered. Curt Powell, at left, had to roll up the sleeves of his jacket so he could play lead guitar. Others from left are Jerry Haacke, Myron, Barry Andrews, and Dick Robinson at the Arkota Ballroom in Sioux Falls.

The Caddies were featured at this 1959 Thursday night Teen Hop at the Arkota Ballroom in Sioux Falls. The big band sound of Pete Erickson was scheduled for the Arkota on the following Wednesday.

concoctions. He was not only a great pizza maker, but a great guy as well. Although he was only about 30 years old, he had white hair. And for some unknown reason, I still remember that he drove a 1954 Corvette. I probably remember that because at the time, as a footsore teenager, I held cars in high esteem, right up there with good pizza.

Thanks to KIHO, I was able to meet Ki-Ho Helgie, whose name in the Sioux Falls phone book was listed as Bob Helgeson. He started in Sioux Falls radio in April 1948 doing the sign-on for KISD, and then spent six years at KSOO playing big band records. From there, he says he was "enticed" to move to KIHO and help with its new format that was sweeping the radio world called the "Top Forty," which was a numbered rating of the latest songs sweeping America, from number one on down to number forty. As part of his KIHO duties, he was also the master of ceremonies at the station's events the Arkota Ballroom called Teen Hops, where we Caddies often played. I got to know him through that outlet. One night after we finished our set at the Arkota, I worked up enough nerve to ask Helgie (then I called him Mr. Helgeson) if he would consider being our manager. Helgie knew the big band era from top to bottom.

He invited me down to the station the next day to talk about the managerial offer. Fortunately for me and for The Caddies, he accepted. He was soon helping with our promotions and handling the other day-to-day, often humdrum, details as more and more people began to call for performance dates and other matters. He recorded on tape a song I'd written, called "Rona Baby," that was later made into a record, and he took snippets of that song to play as background for thirty-second radio advertisements he worked up pitching the play dates of The Caddies.

The Caddies were frequent entertainers at the Arkota Ballroom traditional Thursday night Teen Hop in Sioux Falls. Here they entertain at the event sponsored by KIHO Radio, and emceed by the station's Ki-Ho Helgie, in 1959. Helgie became the group's first manager. From left are Barry Andrews, Jerry Haacke, Myron (with white coat), Dick Robinson on the drums, and lead guitarist Curt Powell, far right.

Myron and two fans at the Prom Ballroom in St. Paul, MN, when he was there in 1959 promoting his new record "Rona Baby."

Jeno's Pizza was just getting started in the growing pizza market in 1959 and used the Myron Lee appearance at the Prom Ballroom in St. Paul to help introduce its product to all of the teens who came to meet and listen to Myron.

Fans, managers, and promoters all turned out in 1959 when Myron was featured at the Prom Ballroom as part of his promotion of the new record "Rona Baby," which reached number ten on the Top Forty list. Standing behind some of the adoring fans are, from left, Mr. and Mrs. Fred Steveken, owners of HEP Records; Jimmy Thomas, Myron's new booker; Myron; Bob Helgeson, former Sioux Falls radio disc jockey and Myron's out-going manager who had moved to the Twin Cities area; and Mory Steinman, a film and entertainment promoter.

Once, when our drummer was ill, we even asked Helgie to go with us to Ruskin Park for a dance we'd signed to do. Helgie had played drums for some of the big bands in Sioux Falls, and he did just fine with us, except that I had to keep reminding him that with rock and roll music, the drummer had to be loud.

I have Helgie to thank for spreading word about us in our formative time. One day he was visiting with a film and show business public relations man, Mory Steinman, from the Twin Cities, who had been introduced to him by Cliff Knoll, manager of the State Theater in Sioux Falls. Helgie told Mory about our group and waxed eloquent about our local successes. Mory told Helgie to bring me up to the Twin Cities to meet him.

So with Helgie's help and good taste, I bought a new suit and one of those narrow ties popular then, and we headed up to the Cities to see Mory. That led to an on-air appearance at WCCO TV, and that evening I was featured at a big teen hop in St. Paul with Bill Diehl at the famed Prom Ballroom. It was the first time teenage girls screamed and yelled as I lip-synced one of my songs. Helgie was a great help in those early years of our band. He was with us for two great years. I was crushed when he left Sioux Falls for work in Minneapolis with Northern States Power Company. He now lives in Bloomington, MN, and remains a valued and good friend.

With our work at the Stardust fading as fall approached, I got a call from Johnny White, the owner of the Cabana Club on Phillips Avenue. He said he'd heard about the crowds we were bringing to the Stardust. He wanted to hire us for the winter months of 1959. We were all still in high school and his offer presented a quandary for us. Staying out until the wee hours on a weekday was not a formula for academic success. But I figured we could handle it and gladly accepted the invitation.

The pay each of us received—$15—was the same we'd received at the Stardust. But we'd added a sax man, Barry Andrews, and were now a five piece band, so Johnny White had to pay $75 total. Since the Cabana sold hard liquor, and because we were underage, the law required that we have an adult along as a chaperone when we were at the Cabana. That problem was easily solved. My mother wrote a note to Johnny, telling him it was okay for us to be there, and asking Johnny to keep an eye on us.

At the Stardust, and then again at the Cabana, our repertoire hinged on the latest top forty hits that Helgie was playing. So we tuned in to KIHO to plan our Wednesday evening selections. We picked the songs we felt comfortable doing, and the ones we knew others liked, and played them by ear after listening to them once or twice.

Of course, the fans that we had entertained at The Stardust Club were now eager to pay the dollar cover charge to elbow into the Cabana every Wednesday night. We packed the place, much to the delight of Johnny White. It soon became necessary for him to hire bouncers to guard the door and keep the peace. Once the place was filled to the limit established by the Fire Marshal, which was about 250, no one else was allowed in until someone inside left. With such an enthusiastic, boisterous, appreciative audience, we were having the time of our lives. The

Still a student at Washington High School in Sioux Falls, Myron Lee and the Caddies were packing them in at the Cabana Club in Sioux Falls. This picture was taken the night in 1959 when big-band director Jimmy Thomas came from Luverne, MN, to listen to the band to decide if he wanted to be their booking agent. From left are Dick Robinson, Myron, and Barry Andrews.

This is the first professionally-taken photograph of Myron Lee and the Caddies in 1958. From left are Barry Andrews, Dick Robinson on drums, Myron, Curt Powell, and Jerry Haacke.

Cabana wasn't a dive, by any means, and it didn't attract a particularly rough crowd, but the inevitable fight would often erupt. When a disturbance like that happened out beyond the stage lights, we continued to play, perhaps with a little more gusto, until the bouncers were able to calm the combatants and escort them to the door.

At that time I was a senior in high school. It was then, and I'm sure it still is, very difficult for any high school senior to haul themselves out of bed weekday mornings. I was also handicapped because we played at the Cabana until the early morning, and might not hit the hay until 3 a.m. before a wake-up call at 7 a.m. To make my early morning reveille even more challenging, I had met a beautiful blonde named Carole, my future wife. Our romance also cut deeply into my sleep schedule.

By early spring 1959, because of the hectic pace and after making every effort to include school in my schedule, I could see the handwriting on the wall, or the blackboard as it were. I dropped out of high school in May, just weeks before graduation. Perhaps I should have stuck around, just in case. But I simply could not keep up with classroom demands and the schedule that now included playing dances several nights each week.

The success our band was experiencing made the decision easy for me. Much later, however, I often wished I could have graduated with my classmates. As it turned out, as I mentioned, my eventual "graduation" was much more auspicious. Washington High classmate George Mickelson was elected governor in 1987. He and his wife Linda were at our class' thirtieth reunion in 1989, and George presented me with a special high school diploma. I was touched and honored, particularly because of the man who called me to the stage. He was a wonderful public servant and a good friend. Sadly, George was killed in an airplane crash on April 19, 1993, returning from government business in Ohio.

In 1959, all I could think about was music. I was making about ten thousand dollars a year during my senior year in high school, which was much more than many people with families were making for their forty or fifty hour work week.

Often in class after a long night on the stage, I would doze off. One day when I fell asleep in class, the teacher, Barney Kremer, told the rest of his attentive students not to disturb me. "Let him sleep," he told them, "he's making way more money than I am." Even the chortles from my classmates didn't awaken me.

At the Washington High School Class of 1959 reunion in 1989, Gov. George Mickelson of the Class of 1959 presented an honorary Washington High School diploma to Myron.

By now the band had changed. Dick Robinson, our drummer, felt that his college studies took precedence over his music, and he left us. He was succeeded by new drummer Dick Davie, who was a classmate of mine at Washington High School. Curt Powell joined us as lead guitar. He was excellent at what he did and I still believe that he was light years ahead of anyone that I have ever heard then or now. Curt and I met at a local talent show. After I heard him play I knew instantly that he was tailor-made for our band.

Jerry Haacke, who had gotten me going on the guitar, moved to electric bass and Barry Andrews, also a Washington High School student, was playing the sax. Barry was a great showman and a big favorite on stage. One of his on-stage antics was to lie on his back, kick his legs in the air and do his seemingly effortless saxophone solos. I continued as the group's singer and also played rhythm guitar. There were now five of us. We were extremely busy. And we were all still very green and sopping wet behind the ears.

I had written two new songs. One was "Rona Baby." The name Rona was the name of the sister of drummer Dick Robinson. (I wonder where she is today?) The other song was "To Be Alone." I received help with the words to this one from my girlfriend Carole. I was proud of these two songs so we packed them up one day, hopped into my 1955 Ford with our equipment trailer bringing up the rear, and

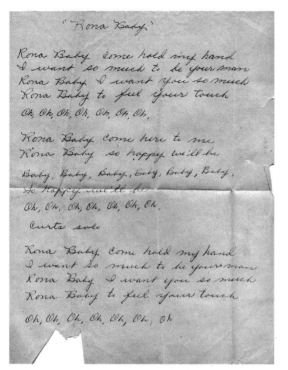

Myron wrote "Rona Baby" early in his career. It was recorded in 1958. This copy of the words and the musical chart were sent to Washington, D. C. in order to obtain a copyright.

headed for St. Paul and the HEP Record Studio.

The HEP "studio" turned out to be something less than what we expected. It was in a cavernous old warehouse that was long past its time. The studio equipment consisted of two Ampex recorders. The label owner Fred Steveaken was there to keep everything running smoothly and to help a sleepy engineer if need be. It was a chilly fall day and the place, of course, wasn't heated. It must have been about fifty degrees inside. We had difficulty playing our instruments because of the chill, but we made it through.

Interestingly, one of Steveaken's big recorders was strategically placed in the room with us, and the other was propped up in the ladies bathroom a few feet away. Steveaken explained that by feeding our sound from the first Ampex to the second recorder, they were able to achieve the echoing sound delay on the records, which was in vogue in those days. Although the layout of the jury-rigged system wasn't perfect, we ended up with a much better sound than the first time we had a recording made on tape at the University of South Dakota.

Steveaken apparently liked what he had heard during our session. He told others about us and was successful in getting our record played on radio stations throughout the Midwest. "Rona Baby" became the most popular side, hitting the charts in places like Fargo, Minneapolis, and Omaha, as well as on good old faithful KIHO in Sioux Falls, where they played the living heck out of it.

While radio stations were giving us mention and play, I was somewhat disappointed that despite our musical successes, the Sioux Falls newspaper, the *Argus Leader*, seemed to be ignoring us. So I wrote a letter to the editor. In it I admonished the newspaper for its usually negative reporting of teenagers, pointing out the bad things they did while ignoring the good. I wrote about the "clean cut" group of Washington High School musicians who were making a name for themselves. I signed a fictitious name and sent it off. About a week later an *Argus*

This picture of Myron Lee and his new Fender Telecaster guitar won a first place state award for the photographer at Harold's Photography in Sioux Falls.

Leader reporter called and asked to meet me for an interview. He wrote a nice story, which I appreciated very much.

About this time in my career, a few months before Bob Helgeson left us, more good fortune came my way in the person of Jimmy Thomas. He was an accomplished drummer in his forties, and the leader of a big band called The Jimmy Thomas Orchestra. Jimmy and his group had played ballrooms throughout the Midwest. He knew the music business and was on a first name basis with all of the ballroom owners and everyone else in the music business. Since the tidal wave of rock and roll music was by now nudging out the big band sound that Jimmy was so adept at making, he was having difficulty finding dates. In fact, his business was in a downward spiral.

His wife Harriet encouraged him to find a real job, we often joked. So he sought me out. He and Harriet had heard about the crowds we were attracting in the Sioux Falls area. At Harriet's stern insistence, Jimmy came to the Cabana one night to check us out and to talk to me about booking my band. It was either that, he joked to me later, or getting a job on the kill floor at the John Morrell Packing Plant in town.

Jimmy, if the truth were known, hated rock and roll with a passion. He often said that his aversion to rock and roll made it difficult for him to decide which would be worse, rock and roll music or the slaughter house. Thankfully for us, he opted for the music and hoped he could learn to like it. Eventually, the rock and roll sound did win Jimmy over.

So one Wednesday night Jimmy came to the Cabana Club to see just what these young punks were all about. Later, he jokingly told me that all he heard there was a "bunch of loud noises." But he was impressed with the packed house and the enthusiastic crowd. He said he hadn't seen anything like that out on his big band circuit for a very long time.

This was the Top Forty Hit listing in 1959, when Myron's song "Rona Baby" was number ten. Fats Domino's "When The Saints Go Marching In" was that week's number twenty-six.

He briefly told me what he had in mind that night, and we arranged to meet the next day to talk business. Because I was underage, Jimmy correctly insisted that my mother be present when we got down to the meat and potatoes. His insistence that Mom be involved impressed me. Let's face it, there were and still are shysters out there in the music business just as there are in any other vocation. Jimmy wasn't one of them. He was sincere, genuine, and always honest to the core, even when it hurt me to hear what he had to say. Mom and I listened as Jimmy related his experience in the music business and how, with his contacts, he was quite certain that after school was out in the spring, he could keep The Caddies busy five or six nights a week.

I was all ears. I asked Jimmy how much he thought I could make after expenses. He thought it could be in the neighborhood of $150 a week. I did a double take and swallowed hard. One Hundred And Fifty Dollars A Week! No one in my family had ever, ever made that kind of money. From the perspective of a 17-year-old, it was a fortune. But Mom urged caution and asked for time to think it over. We told Jimmy we'd get back to him.

A couple of days later I called Jimmy and told him that we liked what he had presented. Mom and I agreed to sign a five-year contract. Of course, Mom did the actual signing since I was still too young. I remember thinking at the time that five years was a very long time. There are no guarantees in life or in musical tastes and preferences. I frankly had no idea that our type of music would remain in the spotlight for even the half a decade stipulated in the contract.

Included in the agreement was the stipulation that Jimmy's contact and dealings with our band would be funneled through me and me alone. He said he wanted it this way because, from his experience, members of any band, including The Caddies, would come and go. I was the only constant. For that reason, he wanted to deal only with me. Jimmy told me that I needed to treat the band as a business. I therefore paid each band member by check, deducting for social secu-

Myron Lee and the Caddies in 1959, while most of them were still students at Washington High School. From left, Jerry Haacke, Barry Andrews, Dick Davie, Myron Lee, and Randy Charles.

rity and other appropriate taxes. I hired Maxine's Bookkeeping Service in Sioux Falls to do my books. Maxine Buskohl performed her responsibilities admirably until she passed away a few years ago. Now, her daughter Connie carries on for me in my business dealings. I have therefore depended on Maxine and now Connie for nearly 45 years.

He also suggested that the group's name be more personally associated to me. Jimmy told me that my name was important and that it should be the cornerstone. He said that co-op bands, like any business, don't usually last too long. He said I needed one person to run the show. He used Lawrence Welk as an example. He told me that people paid to see Lawrence Welk because people knew he would always have a good band. They never inquired about who the drummer was, or who was playing the horn. In the public's eye, he said—as an example—as long as Lawrence Welk was there, that was the secret for his band's success.

I started to think about a name for our group. Myron Wachendorf and the the Caddies seemed to lack a certain pizzazz. Wachendorf also had too many letters to comfortably fit in a newspaper advertisement or on a cardboard poster. And with a name like that, people might identify us as a polka band, not that there's anything wrong with polka music. I like it, but can't play it. So the family name was set aside. I finally decided on the name that, surprisingly, people still remember.

We became Myron Lee and the Caddies. I picked "Lee" because it was short, easy to say and remember, and because of my admiration for a popular singer at that time named Brenda Lee.

I was embarrassed and uncomfortable when I told my buddies and Caddie compatriots that I was going to put my name out front. But there was never a problem. Jimmy was absolutely right in his insistence that we adopt a new name. Just as he had predicted, most of the band members at that time eventually developed other plans for their lives, including college or being drafted into the Army. Over the years, dozens of musicians became part of the band, then left for other pursuits.

When the Myron Lee Fan Club was organized, its first member was Carole Fredrickson. She's kept her membership card all these years and is now Mrs. Myron (Lee) Wachendorf.

Another change we made when Jimmy joined us was to increase the pay for the band members. They would be paid $25 for each performance. It was my responsibility to take care of all of their expenses on the road. After their pay and expenses were deducted, Jimmy and I would split the rest, provided anything remained in the kitty.

I considered myself then, so far as music was concerned, as an energetic, self-assured, high achiever. I wanted to be the best that I could be and I was willing to work and sacrifice to reach that goal. But Jimmy was a leveler and a Godsend for me. His experience and good advice were very important in what I achieved as our band grew in popularity. I don't believe I could have had a career in music if it had not been for him. He knew the "ins and outs" and he knew the ropes of a tricky business where you are often negotiating with complete strangers miles away.

Sometimes, payment is in cash based on admission figures, which can be manipulated. I was young and immature, but I thought that I was a pretty good busi-

An advetising flyer for a Teen Hop at the Arkota Ballroom in Sioux Falls from the early 1960s. Murray Killum's "Long Tall Texan" was then a top ten hit. The Caddies backed up Killum and played for the dance.

nessman and a bandleader. I still believe my best attributes were managing the business and providing band leadership. But frankly, it would have taken me decades to learn all of the idiosyncrasies and minutiae of show business that Jimmy carried around in his shirt pocket. He was such a big help. Most importantly, he was like a father to me.

I had a lot to learn about money management and business. Coming from a background such as mine, I always related success to big cars. The ultimate symbol of success was a white Cadillac. In the fall of 1961, when I turned twenty-one, I bought one with a sticker price of $6,000 at Schoon Motors in nearby Luverne, MN. I traded my Oldsmobile with its 125,000 of mostly highway miles, and I financed the rest. That meant a monthly payment of $250.

After I bought the beautiful new car, I drove it home to show to my mother. She was impressed, but inquired about the cost. Her second question was to ask how I intended to pay for it. She had a point. But I assured her that the band was going places and someday soon I'd be making bushel baskets of money. After showing the car to my mother, I drove to Parker for Grandma Mary to see. She didn't seem all that impressed with it, either.

My next step was to have our equipment trailer painted white to match the Cadillac. I hired Shorty Graff, a sign painter, to garnish the trailer's sides with "Myron Lee and the Caddies."

Money was rolling in. I was young and making more than anyone in my family had ever earned. I was also very naïve. Both my dear mother and my booking agent Jimmy Thomas warned me of the dangers of being too overconfident and reminded me of my pell-mell spending habits. But I thought I knew better. No one could tell me how to live my life. What did they know? Well, I later learned that they knew a heck of a lot more than I did.

I continued to spend lavishly. In between music dates I took trips and lived, as we Dakotans are fond of saying, high off the hog. I bought the most expensive of everything and lived like a king. The first inkling I had that my financial situation was less than admirable was in 1962 when I discovered I had been spending more than I had been taking in. I'm not certain if the situation dawned on me when I learned that I owed the Internal Revenue Service $1,700, or when it became

For their 1962 coast to coast Canadian tour with Buddy Knox, Myron had suits custom made at Crawfords Men's Store in Sioux Falls, then went to Gene's Studio in Sioux Falls for this picture. From left are Fred Scott, Jerry Haacke, Chico Hajek, Randy Charles and Myron, who wore the latest in footwear.

increasingly more difficult to find enough to make my $250 payments each month for my ponderous but purring Cadillac.

The burr under my roaming saddle for the moment were those $250 Cadillac payments. So with the Cadillac albatross around my neck and the IRS breathing down it, I was pleased the day I got to know Ed Paul, who was president of the local musicians union. I told him about the financial hole I was digging for myself. He responded with fatherly advice and I've never forgotten what he told me.

"Dump the Cadillac."

Ed had the financial credentials. He was a wealthy man, probably in his fifties at the time, and he had wisely invested in rental property. Sioux Falls was growing, and there were investment opportunities aplenty, he told me. Ed had also gotten in the drive-in movie business. He built the first drive-in theater in Sioux Falls in the 1940s. It was called Soo Dell Drive-In out on Highway 77 north of the city just north of where Cliff Avenue and Interstate 90 now intersect. It is now a trailer home park.

Ed took a liking to me, and I to him, and we became fast friends. We talked many times about how I needed to turn my life around and change my elaborate spending habits. I took his advice and learned how to make money work for me rather than against me. I gritted my teeth and closed my eyes and got rid of that glorious Cadillac that I'd put over 100,000 miles on in less than a year of road trips.

After that, Jimmy Thomas went with me to the Ford dealer on Eighth and Dakota Avenue and arranged a lease on a new 1963 red Ford station wagon. It was a Country Squire model that had an exterior finish of simulated wood on the sides. I thought it was classy, although today it would probably be considered a typical Ward Cleaver car.

With guidance from Ed Paul, I began salting away a little cash each week and was soon able to repay the IRS. Before much longer, I had $2,000 free and clear. With it I made a down payment to Ed on a three-unit apartment on Eighth and Summit, with the remainder on a contract for deed. The income from two of the apartments was enough for me to make the contract payments and the other provided cash so I could put in a basement apartment, where Carole and I lived after we were first married. When we finally sold it, I made $5,000 in profit, enough for a down payment on a new three bedroom ranch style home on the west side.

About 1970, I bought another six-unit apartment from Ed and he again trusted me with a contract for deed. I fixed the place up and in just a few months I put it on the market. The profit from it was over $15,000. In the mid 1970s I joined with two friends of mine and we bought eight newer duplex units on the west side next to where Carole and I lived.

Ed Paul turned my life around. He taught me to invest at least part of my income in something that makes money, not in something that takes money. I've often thought that schools should offer the Ed Paul Course on money handling. I know it sure worked for me. Ed died a few years ago at the age of 92, but he remains alive in my mind and I think about him almost every day.

5

On the Road

By the spring of 1959, Jimmy Thomas had us booked solid for the summer. We traveled the highways and byways throughout the Midwest. It was an exciting, fast-moving, electrifying time for us. We attracted large crowds everywhere we went. My recording of "Rona Baby" was getting plenty of airtime on radio stations all over the place, and that didn't hurt our notoriety, either.

As we started our summer tour, I came to realize that our niche was in the dance band category rather than as a show band. We were good musicians, but nothing flashy. I had the final say on the music we played and I insisted that everything had a good dance beat to it and was recognizable. I sometimes cringe today when I read about some of the young bands getting started. Most of them could use a Jimmy Thomas in their midst to teach them what they should be doing. It's no wonder many of the groups end as a mere flash in the pan. These days I often hear the term "cover bands," or bands that play other people's hit songs. It's mentioned or written about as if it is a "lesser" band that lacks originality. But I see nothing wrong with cover bands. There is no written or unwritten law that prevents them from repeating what others are doing. Show me a group that plays primarily the songs that the band members have written, or obscure album tracks, and I'll show you a group that is probably in the business temporarily, for fun of hearing their own songs, rather than in it for business. Usually they don't last very long.

I'm proud that we always gave the people what they liked to dance to and what they liked to hear. We had some original stuff, too, but most of our efforts were to entertain. Sure, we clowned around a little bit, but mostly we played for the people who loved to dance. If a particular tune didn't attract dancers to the floor, it was soon gone from our repertoire. Our songs—and in the early days we had a couple hundred of them memorized—were nearly always taken from the top forty music charts of the week.

Early in our relationship, Jimmy advised me to plan each evening so that when the dance was over, we would leave the crowd wanting more. Therefore, our selection of songs was designed to keep the dance floor full. For our evening's finale, I tried to pick a song that everyone knew well and loved to hear.

Another reason many musical groups lack longevity, in my humble opinion, is because they are over-managed, with too many bosses, and because they often play for their own enjoyment rather than for the people out front on the dance floor who paid to get in. They forget why they are on stage in the first place.

There's more to running a successful band than one would think. The selection of the music is a big part. We hit the road with about two hundred songs in our repertoire, but the trick was to select the songs and their sequence for the particular audience. Some bands played the same songs in the same sequence night after night. I tried to keep our presentations new and fresh and custom made for the time, place, and people for whom we were playing. The crowd at Ruskin Park might be just slightly different than the people who drove to Fargo to dance to our music. I learned to read an audience quite well, and after a few false starts, to give them what they wanted.

Most of the ballrooms or clubs we played during that time were built in the 1920s before The Crash, when the nation was aglow financially, and before it started to sink into the quagmire known as the Dust Bowl and the Depression Years. The halls were large, wooden structures with the dance floor in the center, surrounded by straight-backed, wooden booths or wooden benches lining the outside walls. They were uncomfortable for a long sit, but perhaps designed that way so that people got up and danced to give their backside a break.

Because they were built before air conditioning, many had huge window coverings of board siding that could be folded down on hinges during the evening to allow the cool breezes to flow through the screens. But even that didn't cool things down too much, and with the added heat of the stage lights and amplifiers, we were usually wringing wet by closing time. The breezes also helped clear away the cigarette smoke, which curled and wafted in great abundance in those days.

Speaking of stage lights, when we first got started I noticed that no one used lights other than what was available at the ballroom or club, and they were usually inadequate for anything but preventing pratfalls and tripping over equipment. I think we were the first band in the Midwest to carry colored floodlights with us that were intended for ambiance. We placed them in the front and back of the stage to enhance the look and atmosphere. I had stands with colored lights inside made on which we set our amps. In my opinion, lighting helps set the mood and improves the appearance of the stage.

Many of the ballrooms had the ubiquitous mirrored ball slowly rotating on its axis in the center of the ceiling, reflecting the light in random patterns. I remember the Japanese Gardens in Flandreau, SD, had an old rotating mirrored ball that they told us was handmade by slathering Plaster of Paris on a basketball and then sticking the small mirrors from discarded women's rouge and powder containers for the reflectors. Surprisingly, that dance hall is still standing and is still used from time to time. I assume the old mirrored basketball is still spinning, too. Sadly, most of

After Myron hired Jimmy Thomas as his booking agent in 1959, this was the large poster made to promote the band. Dozens would be placed at appropriate spots within fifty miles of the ballroom where they were scheduled to appear.

the old wooden structures have succumbed to wind and fire or to progress. Very few of the dance halls we played remain standing today. The Groveland Park Ballroom near Tyndall, where we played our first out of town dance as a fill-in during the big band's breaks, is still around. However, I'm told it is now a machine shed.

Many of the ballroom operators were middle-aged survivors of these difficult times in the 1930s, probably holding two jobs, and they had a tuba full of experience at what they did. Some knew how to fudge a little and to take advantage of the visiting bands as a way of holding down their expenses or upping their take from admissions. And naturally, being good businessmen and women, they wanted to pay the bands as little as possible. The opportunists were in the minority on the dance hall circuit, but just in case, we had Jimmy out front watching over our interests and keeping an eagle eye on the ticket booth. So we felt secure in our dealings.

We often played at Al Kirby's famous and venerable Hollyhock Ballroom in Hatfield, MN. Kirby must have made a fortune for years from the big bands that he was able to bring in. Like so many other ballroom managers by the time my band came along, he reluctantly accepted the fact that the era of the big band was ending. Crowds had also dwindled because of television and a host of other entertainment choices. Some Saturday nights, there were more big band members on stage than dancers on the floor. So even though Kirby and many others like him may have had a certain disdain for the brash youngsters wearing narrow neckties who brought rock and roll music to town, they were smart enough to know that they needed bands such as ours to help them pay their bills.

When we played at the Hollyhock, Jimmy would offer Kirby two choices for payment. He could book the band for a flat $250 for the night. The other option was that the ballroom manager could gamble and sign on for a smaller guaranteed of one hundred twenty-five dollars, or sixty percent of the gate, whichever was greater. It seemed that most ballroom managers opted for the percentage of gate, and that's what Kirby did the first time we played there in May1959. We had quite a fan following by then, even in the Hatfield area. Nearby KLOH of Pipestone played our songs regularly, and that helped with the Minnesota crowds. It was a very popular station with the kids then, and even those in Sioux Falls tuned in to listen to KLOH music.

We packed them into the Hollyhock like peas in a pod. People lined up at the ticket booth while a smiling Kirby worked inside the ticket booth, raking in the dough. Unknown to Kirby, or anyone for that matter, Jimmy was usually nearby, as he always was, with a little thumb-operated counter in his pocket. I need to point out that Kirby was an honest man and a good operator and we never had any trouble with his ticket sale count. But that wasn't necessarily the case with all dance hall managers.

Since the tickets most often used by dance hall operators came in a plate-sized roll and were sequentially numbered, Jimmy might pop his head into the booth after about fifteen minutes of sales, slap the ticket seller on the back and comment about how good business was. Then, nonchalantly, he'd pull that little counter from his pocket, glance at it and comment, almost to himself, about the number of ticket sales the counter showed. It was a little ploy Jimmy used to help keep things in the ticket booths on the up and up, just in case. From time to time, Jimmy might discover that a ballroom manager had fiddled with a roll of tickets, inserting others with different sequential numbers somewhere inside the roll. Using the numbers of these "extra tickets," the manager might be able to furnish attendance figures that did not reflect actual sales.

That first job at the Hollyhock earned us about $600 as our sixty percent of the take. Years later, I used the percentage share idea in Hurley, SD, and the result was the largest payday ever for me. Though the years, we brought huge crowds to the Hollyhock. In the 1960s, we probably played there thirty or forty times and some of those gigs broke the house attendance records. I have fond memories of the Hollyhock, which is now gone, and I have equally great and lasting memories of good old Al Kirby. I'll have more to say about the Hollyhock later.

The best advertising, it is said, is by word of mouth. And that's true. If people like something, they tell their friends and the crowds grow with each return engagement. But as Jimmy warned, you can wear thin on a crowd, too. There can be too much of a good thing. So we tried to return to venues every five or six weeks, rather than every weekend. By the fall of 1959, Jimmy had worked out a schedule that took us to five states: Iowa, North and South Dakota, Minnesota, and Nebraska.

With all of that travel by car, it was Jimmy who thought of every contingency out on the road. He even advised me on what I should do if, late at night out on the road, our car ran short on gas somewhere. His advice came in handy one night returning from a dance at Ruskin Park. We were hurried leaving Sioux Falls for the job ninety miles away and I forgot to fill the Cadillac with gas. Returning to Sioux Falls after the dance, the gauge was flirting with empty. It was about 3 a.m. and in the small towns between Ruskin and Sioux Falls, everything was rolled up and put to bed. But I remembered that Jimmy had advised me that if I should be in need of gas early in the morning out in the boondocks when everything was closed up, I should cruise through the town until I found its night watchman or cop. All of the towns at that time had someone awake and watching during the night, he told me, and they had keys to gas pumps or knew where the station owner lived, to meet just such emergencies.

We pulled into a small town, I forget which one, and drove around until we found the night policeman. He was able to see to it that we got some gas. He also asked us if we'd been drinking. I told him that we had, and that we'd played earlier that night at Ruskin Park. I handed him five dollars for the gas, he wished us well and advised me to "drive carefully." I doubt if a scene like that would happen today.

In 1960, when I was nineteen, Jimmy's management expertise was becoming well known by others in the music business. He branched out and leased the Showboat Ballroom in Lake Benton, MN. Later, he also ran the ballroom in Milltown in Hutchinson County near the Parker of my youth. Speaking of Milltown, I once received a nice birth announcement from a couple whose names now escape me. They wrote on the card how happy they were with their new baby, and mentioned that by counting back from the child's birth date, they had concluded that the Milltown parking lot during one of our performances there was where their new family had actually gotten started. They said they gave the baby the middle name of Myron in my honor. It was one of the nicest birth announcements I've ever received.

Jimmy also started to book other rock and roll bands and to attract big name stars to the Midwest, which, by the way, is an ideal place where fading stars can find both enthusiastic fans and good work. People out here think nothing of driving fifty miles for a coffee break or a movie and I honestly believe that they might drive even further for a dance or to listen to a big star, no matter the state of his or her career.

Jimmy often booked our band along with established stars such as Tommy Rowe or other big name recording artists who might not be traveling with a regular band. When that happened, we were often given the honor of serving as their backup band. Jimmy would arrange a tour of ten or twelve nights and that gave us more exposure as well as the opportunity to work with the big names in the business.

Jimmy soon organized the Thomas Booking Agency headquartering in Luverne, MN. His reputation grew and his phone was ringing off the wall. Buddy Knox, often seen in the 1950s and 1960s on the *Steve Allen Show* and on the popular *Ed Sullivan Show*, was one of those who sought out the organizational expertise of Jimmy. Buddy had several big hits like "Party Doll," which he also wrote, and others like "Hula Love," "Rock Your Little Baby to Sleep," and "Somebody Touched Me in the Dark Last Night."

When Jimmy first met Buddy at the ballroom on Lake Madison (SD) in 1959, Buddy was more or less down on his luck, nearly broke and struggling to keep his career above water. After his show at the Madison ballroom, Jimmy sought Buddy out and asked him if he would be interested in more Midwestern show dates. He told him the opportunities were limitless in the Midwest. A few days later, they worked out an arrangement, and I didn't know it at the time, but that agreement had an eventual impact on the success of Myron Lee and the Caddies, too.

Over the next few years, the upper Midwest became a hot spot for Buddy. I remember that while his band rode from one job to the next in a car pulling the equipment trailer, Buddy tooled along in a big, black, seemingly block-long 1957 Lincoln Continental Mach IV that he'd purchased from Julie London ("Cry Me A River") when he worked with her in New York. Despite the outward appearance of success personified by that big Julie London car, one day Jimmy noticed that the car's tires were lacking any semblance of treads. Jimmy, perhaps to protect his investment, had to loan Buddy enough money to buy a new set of tires.

Jimmy had a great run in the 1960s with his ballrooms and his booking agency. I've often thought that our paths must have been meant to cross, perhaps decreed by the stars or something, because without him to help me along, and without me to help him avoid the kill floor of the John Morrell plant, who knows what our lives might have been like.

And thanks to Jimmy, we were about to hit it lucky. The band was soon to be traveling Canada with Buddy Knox in his Julie London car. There was an ice-cold adventure in store for us.

6

On to Flin Flon

As the Sixties began, the band was busy and we were having a ball working almost every night and sleeping well into the day. From my date book I kept at the time, for the first week in May 1960, we had the following engagements and were paid the following amounts:

May 2, Ravina, $125; May 3, Club Cabana, $80; May 4, Centerville, $140; May 5, Ruskin Park, $135; May 6, Rest Haven, $160; and Saturday night, May 7, Dell Rapids, $271.

For one busy period at the end of 1962 we spent Christmas Day in Mitchell, $411; Dec. 26, Winner, $125; Dec. 27, Hot Springs, $325; Dec. 28, Ft. Dodge, $175; Dec. 29, Swisher, $250; Sunday, Dec. 30, Lake View, $188; and New Year's Eve 1962 at the Sioux Falls Coliseum with Bobby Vinton. Interestingly, I have marked that date down in my book as a financial "loss."

But despite that minor setback, which I'll talk about later, the Sixties would bring us our biggest breaks, thanks to Buddy Knox and a North Dakota singer and performer named Bobby Vee.

As the new decade began I had purchased a new Oldsmobile Fiesta station wagon for $5,000. The car had all the bells and whistles, from air conditioning to air shocks, so we could handle the equipment trailer with ease. The problem was that the new-fangled shocks would leak the air that was supposed to cushion us from the bumps. We'd often limp home in the early hours of the morning with the car suspended about three or four inches off the highway. And the ride was bone jarring.

I first met Buddy Knox when he appeared in Sioux Falls. We had played a couple of shows together and he had often told me he loved my band. We got along great even if he was seven years older. Although he was still in his twenties, I kidded with him and called him the Granddaddy of Rock and Roll, and he got a kick out of that. As I got to know him better, Buddy became my idol and role model,

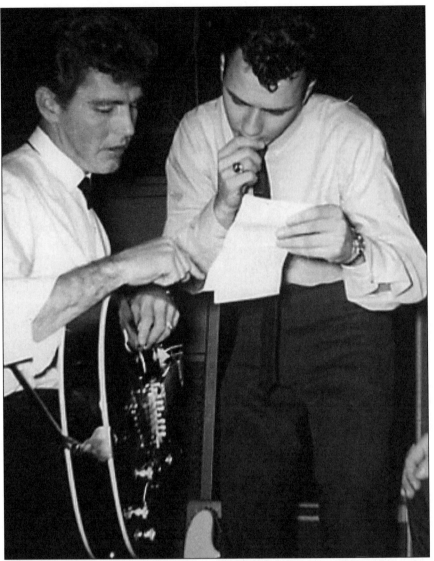

Buddy Knox and Myron review the sequence of Buddy's songs prior to performing during the 1961 Canadian tour.

and it was hard to believe that after watching him on television and buying his records and reading all that I could about him, he and I were now good friends. He gained fame and admiration from fans and from professional musicians, too, because he was the first American to both write and then record a number one rock and roll hit, "Party Doll." It sold millions and was a big hit the world over.

He'd been booked for a three and one-half month, coast-to-coast tour of Canada. The down side was that it would be a winter tour. To my surprise, he told me that he wanted me and my band to join him on what would be the first extended Canadian tour by an American rock and roll group, according to *Billboard Magazine.*

Buddy said he wanted us on the tour with him for several reasons. Of course, he liked the sound of our band, and his had grown weary of the pace and wanted some time off. Besides, Buddy whispered in my ear, his band members wanted too much money to do the tour. So Buddy and Jimmy Thomas worked out a deal. We'd be paid $850 a week and Buddy would take care of hotel and road expenses. Jimmy wasn't all that enamored that we'd be leaving his booking stable for a while, because of the commission money he'd be missing out on.

But I argued that the Canadian tour was an opportunity we had to accept. I finally convinced Jimmy that the trip would in the long run help the band and Jimmy Thomas.

In preparation for the Canadian trip, and with memories of the infamous air shocks on the station wagon, I brought a new, 1960 black Oldsmobile station wagon with a red interior. It was a beauty and would prove to be one of the best cars I ever owned. We pulled out of Sioux Falls bound for the east coast of Canada on Jan 12, 1961. We were excited about the upcoming tour but a little sad to be leaving our friends and families and, for me, my new steady girlfriend Carole. In the Olds with me were Jerry Haacke, bass; Randy Charles, lead; Cal Arthur, sax, and Dick Davie, drums. All were excellent musicians and all were just eighteen years old.

The plan as put together by the promoter of the tour, George Nellis of Moose Jaw, Saskatchewan, was to meet Buddy at St. John's, New Brunswick, which was our first date. The January weather was kind to us all the way to St. John's, but we did notice that the snow piles were considerably larger in Canada than the usual South Dakota variety.

We had worked with Buddy before, so we knew most of his material and the rehearsals went well. The band sounded just great and we all got off on the right foot with the large crowd at the first show of the tour in St. Johns. After that, our little caravan headed west. I drove the black Olds and by now Buddy had a new beige Cadillac DeVille. We must have looked like a classy group as we drove through all those little Canadian towns between tour stops. Everywhere we went the people were extremely friendly and receptive. I got the sense that the Canadians were starved for American entertainment and our shows were well attended.

In Canada, at that time, dancing was not allowed on Sunday. So it was our day of rest, too. But the other six days of the week, Nellis kept us busy. We usually did two shows a day, each lasting two hours. The Caddies led off each show, doing about an hour. After a break, we'd bring Buddy out. He'd sing his big hits "Somebody Touched Me in the Dark Last Night," "Hula Love," and a string of others. Some people in the crowd would dance as we played, but most squeezed in close to the stage to gawk and wave their hands and sing along, similar to what often takes place at performances today, except we didn't have as many security people around as they do now. In fact, most of the time we didn't have any security. But we never had a serious problem.

Between the two shows, we sold eight-by-ten glossies at fifty cents apiece, including one of Buddy and me. After the show when we had more time, we would autograph the pictures for anyone who wished, which was most of the buyers. Profit from the photographs just about covered road expenses, Buddy told me.

Buddy's wife Glenda remained at home in Macon, GA, but from time to time, she joined us on the road for a few days. Her visits inspired me to call Carole, and on one of those calls, Carole told us of the terrible blizzard that was the latest gift to the Dakotas from Canada, so the cold and snow we were experiencing wasn't all that much different than what the folks back home were putting up with.

On stage, my band was decked out in beautiful, black mohair, custom-made suits crafted before we left on the tour by the tailors at Crawford's Menswear in Sioux Falls. Each one cost me $200. We went all out with them, too, even having our names embroidered on the lining of the jackets. The suits glistened in the spotlights and we all thought they were the cat's meow.

Buddy was even more sartorially prepared. He had a rack mounted across the back seat of his Cadillac that was crammed with tailor-made suits and shirts.

I especially remember our date on Prince Edward Island. We drove our cars onto a combination ferry/ice breaker to take us across the bay to the island. The ice was thick and at times the ferry would shudder and stop, then back up and take another run. We saw seals on the ice flow that others aboard said had floated down from Greenland. For kids from South Dakota, we were all eyes on that boat trip.

Approaching Quebec City, the road signs were all in French. We had fun trying to figure out and pronounce what they said, but we were pathetic at French. Somehow, however, we made it to our destination in Quebec City.

When we stayed in hotels, teenage girls would often climb the fire escapes or try other ingenious approaches to try to get a better look at us, and to get into our rooms. It was flattering in a way, but scary, too. In the larger cities, we depended on security and protection from the Royal Canadian Mounted Police.

When we played in the bigger cities like Toronto or Montreal, George Nellis arranged to have other American singing stars in the shows, and that boosted attendance. In Montreal, there was a crowd of over 10,000. The Ventures, with their hit, "Walk Don't Run," helped pack them in. Dion flew up from New York and sang "Runaround Sue" and others. Ersel Hickey killed them with his "Bluebird Over The Mountain."

Bobby Vee, who was hotter than a pistol at the time, drove to Montreal all the way from California with his brother Bill, who was his road manager. Two of his big hits at that time were "Take Good Care of My Baby" and "Devil Or Angel." It was especially good to see Bobby since I had met him many times before when we did dates in his hometown of Fargo, ND. We are the same age, both of us nineteen by that time, but he was making big bucks and we Caddies were splitting $850 a week.

I had assumed Bobby Vee would show up in Montreal driving a big Cadillac, so I was somewhat surprised when he arrived in a new Volkswagon. Bobby not only had an exceptional talent, but he is also a good businessman and a great guy, personable, friendly and interesting to talk to. He was conservative in his outlook and street smart in the business. I liked him. He is still busy in the music business and we remain good friends.

After Bobby and the big names left us in Montreal where we played to that huge crowd of 10,000 people, it was back to our little two-car caravan. The February temperatures in Canada were often down in the 50-below range, before wind chill was factored in, so at most places we stayed they had electrical outlets for our cars' block heaters. The guess and by-golly of knowing each morning that your car was going to start didn't fit well with a show tour schedule. So whenever we could on overnight stays, we rented the bays of a nearby gas station and parked our cars and the trailer inside.

I've played in some very unusual places, but often in Canada, the biggest place in town was the hockey rink, which absolutely wasn't designed for music. Many of our appearances were in those chilly, cavernous arenas. The stage would be set up at one end of the rink and a canvas covering pulled down over the ice up front where people stood to watch and listen. The arenas were cold and damp and they were definitely not our favorite venues. In that kind of environment, it was difficult to keep our instruments in tune.

Our nightly engagements were often 350 to 500 miles apart, so we spent hours of windshield time—frosted-over windshield time, I should say. Usually we'd pack up after the shows while the adrenalin was still flowing, and head out for the next town. We had to keep a sharp eye for meandering moose that might find the highway a good resting place. We always had an abundant supply of cans of fuel additives for emergency starts. The wind blew at one speed only, which was "high," and it built jutting, brick-hard finger drifts on the highway.

The tours were definitely for young people because the hours were long, the pace day-in and day-out was numbing, and the elements could be deadly if one were not careful. Fortunately, we possessed good South Dakota winter sense, so we usually could anticipate the problems we might encounter. We'd check into our motel or hotel early each morning and get as much sleep as time would allow before preparing for the next show.

Often, Buddy would invite me to ride along with him to help drive and keep him awake when he was at the wheel during those all-night journeys. I was, of course, thrilled and honored to ride along. His stories made the time fly by. He'd been around the block and had worked with all of the rock and roll greats. He talked about his army days in a tank division, and he often mentioned his friend Buddy Holly, who, with Richie Valens, who was just 17, and The Big Big Bopper, J. P. Richardson, died in an airplane crash in the early-morning hours of Feb. 3, 1959, eight miles from the Mason City, IA airport.

Both Knox and Holly recorded at the same studio in Clovis, NM. Buddy also had known and worked with Elvis Presley and often reminisced about those days when Buddy was in the army. Elvis was drafted in 1958. Buddy was stationed with him in Texas, and the two became good friends. Later, when Buddy traveled to California to record for Liberty Records, he often called Elvis and would always be invited to visit at Elvis' California home. He told me that once, he drove out to see Elvis at about 10 a.m. and when Elvis came to the door, Buddy was surprised to see that he was heavily made up and was even wearing eye shadow. His hair was dyed jet black. Buddy said he looked like a million dollars. Even early in the morning, Elvis was concerned about how he looked, except, apparently, later in his fading career when drugs transposed him into a bloated caricature of himself.

On one long, cold and snowy ride, Buddy told me that Buddy Holly often reminisced about growing up in Texas, sitting on his front porch in Lubbock and looking at the stars, knowing that something great was going to happen to him and to his music. I knew the dream.

Incidentally, the trio of rock and rollers killed in that plane crash had appeared only hours before at the Surf Ballroom in Clear Lake, IA. The Caddies played there at least twice that I remember. Another similar incident was that I had once flown in foul winter weather from the Spearfish airport despite the sincere and vociferous urgings of Conway Twitty not to do so. Once airborne, I wasn't at all sure we would survive that long flight back to Sioux Falls, either. But we did.

Buddy told me that early in his career, when his "Party Doll" was such a big hit, he took part in the big Alan Freed show in New York. When a young Paul Anka, who would later have the hit "Diana," came on his own to New York from his home in Ottawa, Canada, his parents had given him just $100 spending money. To save his meager purse, Anka stayed with Buddy. Anka slept in Buddy's hotel room bathtub with just one blanket for comfort.

I was shocked when he told about the time some of the big shots at his record company, Roulette, had threatened to kill him. Buddy told me that he had to hire a lawyer to help recover royalties owed from the four million Roulette records he'd

Buddy Knox on stage in Montreal, Canada. Cal Arthur is at left, and beyond Knox are Myron and lead Caddies guitarist, the late Curt Powell.

sold. He told me that one company official in New York asked him strange, subtle questions, such as if he was enjoying the good life and if he would like to continue working. Buddy took it all as a veiled threat, and was sure of it when the man suggested that Buddy drop his legal pursuits. As I became more acquainted with many of the big stars of the day, I was surprised to learn that things like that were not at all uncommon.

It was during one of those long car trips in Canada that Buddy gave me what would usually be good advice, but which turned out to play a part in one of the biggest financial mistakes of my career. Here's how it happened.

As I've mentioned, it was always my intention to play the music people wanted. If we were asked to play something we didn't know, I rushed out the next day and tried to find it in the record shops. We'd listen, and know how to play it by our next dance. That's how I hooked up with the song "Peter Rabbit," the object of my mistake.

At one of our dances, three different kids on three different occasions came up and asked me if we could play the new song "Peter Rabbit." I had never heard of it. But I figured if these kids knew of a good song

This is the control room at the K-Bank recording studio in Minneapolis where Myron recorded his most popular record ever, "Peter Rabbit," in 1962. Note the large Ampex recorder at left.

coming along, I wanted to listen to it and learn to play it. One thing led to another and I ended up getting permission from the writer, the late Tim Smith of Sioux Falls, to record "Peter Rabbit." He agreed. It was a well-done, silly little song, but catchy. We made a quick trip to K-Bank Studios in Minneapolis and in one take had it on tape. I had it pressed on my own label, planning on it to be only a demo. As it turned out, people still equate that song with The Caddies.

Sometime later I received a telephone call from Wink Martindale in California. I recognized the name right away. He had recorded a big hit in the 1950s called "Deck of Cards." He told me he was with DOT Records, then a major label, and he was interested in putting "Peter Rabbit" on the DOT label as a single. He said he'd heard good things about sales on my label from Midwest distributors. He offered me two and one-half cents a copy for the rights. As I talked to Wink, I remembered the advice Buddy Knox had given me on that long Canadian tour.

He'd told me that the record companies would always try to take advantage of singers to get the best deal for the company and not the artist.

Buddy advised me to never accept less than four or five cents a copy for a record. So I told Martindale that I needed at least four cents rather than the two and one-half cents he'd offered. There was a silence, and then he told me he'd have to think about that counter offer. He'd get back to me. Of course, he never did. Several years later, incidentally, a group called Dee Jay and the Runaways of Spirit Lake, IA, took the "Peter Rabbit" song and made it into a big hit. It sold over 400,000 copies. Martindale, incidentally, would later become famous as a television game show host. Of course, cruising across Canada with Buddy Knox was some time before "Peter Rabbit" came into my life.

On the tour, Buddy would faithfully wire money back to his wife Glenda every week. During the week, he was usually paid in cash after each show. On many occasions I saw a non-descript briefcase in the trunk of his car that he told me always had from $10,000 to $20,000 in it representing the week's take.

Buddy was a handsome, suave man and a wonderful singer. Even though his wife Glenda stayed home in Georgia most of the time Buddy was on the road, I never once saw or heard of him cheating on his wife, and Lord knows, he had plenty of chances.

Although the Canadian cities and towns are often few and far between, we never minded the long hours on the road. We were young, we were seeing the world, and we were getting paid for our efforts. Much of the time, everyone in the car caught up on sleep, except the driver. The car radio was always on and we listened to those powerful radio stations that serve Canada and that beamed up across the border from the United States. Radio WSM of Nashville came in strong as an ox and it was one of our favorite spots on the dial. So was KOMA in Oklahoma City and KAAY from Little Rock. We often listened to Wolfman Jack booming in all the way from Del Rio, Texas. We all enjoyed listening to all kinds of music, from county to rock and roll.

Periodically, because of some atmospheric quirk, but much to our pleasure, we could fine-tune the radio dial and pick up KSOO from Sioux Falls. When that happened we all experienced a tinge of homesickness, but we drove on, taking our turn at the wheel and anxious to reach the next stop, a warm bed, and some much-needed rest. The music business is darn hard work. You have to love it to do it over and over again. And we all certainly did enjoy what we were doing, so it was an enjoyable and exciting time for us.

We played Brandon, Manitoba, and then on March 10 headed for Flin Flon, Manitoba, an out-of-this-world place north of everything. Now it is one of the biggest cities in Canada. It was founded in 1920 as a mining community, so when we dropped in, it had only existed for about forty years. The last two hundred miles of the road to Flin Flon when we drove there was graveled, and beyond Flin Flon, there was no road continuing on north at all. It was the end of the line. At Flin Flon, we entertained a small group of about three or four hundred people in the high school gymnasium. But be it Flin Flon or Montreal, the Canadian people were wonderful and appreciative. When we checked into the hotel after that long gravel

In 1961 while on a Canadian tour, three popular singers posed before the Montreal show. Bobby Vee, at left and Dion, at right. Myron still sported the "wet hair" look and what he called his "Bill Haley" forehead curl at the time, but soon discovered the dry hair look used by Vee, Dion, and the other big stars.

road journey, incidentally, I saw my first honest-to-gosh Eskimo in the lobby. Maybe he was a Buddy Knox fan for all I know.

We continued to play our way west across the continent and by March 21 we were in the Province of Alberta playing in cities such as Calgary and Edmonton. My record of "I Need Someone" on a Canadian label was on the charts at that time and we heard it played several times as we drove from town to town. We had also stopped at Moose Jaw, the hometown of the tour's promoter, Mr. Nellis. The last stop of our three and one-half month odyssey was in Vancouver, British Columbia. By then it was mid-April and spring had sprung.

When we arrived in Vancouver, we were not surprised when the motel proprietor, who apparently had seen our equipment trailer that identified us as an American band, declined to provide accommodations. We asked him why and were told that Johnny Cash and his band had literally destroyed a couple of rooms when they were there earlier. Among other things, they had apparently gotten some orange paint somewhere and painted everything, walls, furniture, and the whole nine yards. The motel manager also mentioned Gene Vincent as a troublemaker. I knew that he was also famous among musicians as something of a hell raiser, too. We had apparently followed in the wake of Cash and Vincent across the western part of Canada, and we often encountered difficulties renting rooms because of their partying legacy.

We arranged to stay elsewhere and found Vancouver in the spring to be beautifully adorned with flowers blooming and green grass in great abundance. We were all impressed with the beauty of the city and thankful that our tour was ending. But we had one more concert to go. It would be a memorable one for all of us.

We would be sharing the stage with Johnny Cash, who had been booted out of the motel where we first stopped, and Bob Luman, who was there to sing his hit "Let's Think About Livin'." We met Cash and the others backstage before the show. None of us in my band drank at that time, so our eyes really opened wide when we walked into the dressing room to find Cash, his band, and Luman, huddled and intent around a table playing poker. Huge clouds of cigar and cigarette smoke billowed skyward as they passed around a big bottle of expensive whiskey. They were seasoned veterans, and even with a huge crowd in the auditorium that night, the anticipation of going out before 10,000 fans didn't seem to faze them. They weren't a bit nervous. That wasn't the case with the Caddies. At that stage in our lives and our careers, we were understandably always anxious and pensive before every show. I wondered at the time how Cash and crew could consume alcohol as they did, and then go out and do a show. Years later I would discover, but to a lesser degree, just how it was done.

The tour finally ended and we all had mixed emotions that not only our good times were ending, but our arduous, long trip across Canada, and nightly concert schedule, were coming to a close. Buddy Knox headed south to Los Angeles to record some new songs for Liberty Records. We pointed our faithful Olds toward South Dakota. It was a long, 1,500-mile journey that seemed longer because we so anticipated seeing our loved ones again. In retrospect, those three and one-half months now seem a blur. It is hard to believe that we actually stopped and played at so many places. The trip was good for us to make at that point in our careers, and the experience no doubt helped prepare us for the long, hard road ahead.

Incidentally, Buddy called me again in 1962 and we did a two-week tour in Washington and Oregon with him. We became wonderful friends. Sadly, the kid from Happy, TX, died of cancer on Feb. 4, 1999, and I cried for the loss of my good friend and a very good person. Buddy and I had maintained contact for years. He would call me up from somewhere or another several times a year just to chat, and we always exchanged Christmas cards. I still miss Buddy Knox, and I still listen to "Party Doll."

While meandering across Canada, incidentally, I found a "new look." I noticed that Buddy and the other big stars we played with used makeup for their stage appearances. So I tried it and I liked it. When we left Sioux Falls, I combed my hair in what we called the wet hair look, using plenty of elbow grease to flatten down

During the 1960 tour of Canada, many stars joined Buddy Knox and Myron Lee and the Caddies in Montreal. That's Myron in the center, with, from left, Ersil Hickey, Dion, Lee, Buddy Knox, and Bobby Vee. After observing the clothing styles of the stars, Myron retired his sports jacket soon after this picture was taken.

the locks encumbered with generous doses of Crank's Hair Oil. And I furrowed in a pronounced part on the left side of my head punctuated with some curls cascading casually down on my forehead. Real cool stuff. But we noticed that all of the big stars we worked with were sporting a "dry" look. They used a hair dryer to fluff the hair back so it was nice and full. For one thing, it gives one the false impression that you have a whole lot more hair than could actually be verified by a detailed inventory. When we got back to Sioux Falls, Carole loved my new hair, so I felt vindicated for my experimentation.

We drove into Sioux Falls about 6 p.m. I picked Carole up and that night we went to the Starlite Outdoor Theater, then had a good old American-made pizza. It was good to be back, but my life was on the road, and jobs were waiting.

During the life of the Caddies, we would return often to Canada on tour, but we always seemed to draw the duty in the winter months. In March of 1962, Jimmy Thomas booked us with Dorsey Burnette for a two-week tour north of the border. Burnette had the hits "A Tall Oak Tree" and "Hey, Little One." His brother Johnny was also a singer who had the hit "You're Sixteen, You're Beautiful and You're Mine." Bobby Dylan would later call Dorsey one of the best songwriters ever, and I believe that he was. He wrote for Rickie Nelson and was in great demand by other big stars. Our tour of Canada with Dorsey was mainly in towns in Manitoba and Alberta.

On that chilly tour, Dorsey would do two shows a night and we took care of the dance portion of the evenings, as well as backing him up for his songs. He was nearly thirty years old at that time, and a little on the heavy side. He lacked that pretty boy rock and roll image that others in the business had. I don't believe the "dry hair" look ever caught on with him, either.

During our time together, he told me that he'd like to produce a record with me singing some of his songs. He would pay all of my expenses to Hollywood, where he lived and where we would do the recording. We decided that next spring after the tour ended would be the best time to make the records. So for the remainder of the Canadian tour, whenever we had time, he would take up his guitar and sing material he had written so I could pick out the songs that I liked. By the time our two-week tour was finished, I'd selected four songs that I liked and thought fit my singing style and abilities. Although he told me many times that he was impressed by my band's sound, especially for live shows, he suggested that for the recording session, I should record with a studio band from California that specialized in making records. The bands were comprised of what were known in the business as studio musicians. They knew the nuances and subtleties of studio recording, which is different than playing before a live audience. I felt bad about leaving my band behind, but Dorsey insisted on recording the songs his way. It was also less expensive than flying out my entire band.

When I went to Hollywood to record, I took our new drummer, Chico Hajek, of Tyndall, with me for moral support. We were good buddies. As a hick from the Dakotas, I needed his company out there in tinsel town's fast lane. Chico, by the way, was an excellent musician. He was versatile and could play anything from polkas to jazz. After we got to California, I thought that Carole might enjoy seeing how the recording business works, and so called back to South Dakota and asked her to join us. I sent her airline ticket and I remember the round-trip cost was just $85.

Dorsey had rented the same recording studio that he'd used many times, including recording many of Ricky Nelson's records. He was familiar with the sound there and he liked the engineer who operated the equipment. It was located near the palladium where Lawrence Welk taped his television show.

Dorsey introduced me to the studio musicians he had hired. Earl Palmer was on drums, Joe Osborn was on bass, and James Burton was lead guitar. Both Osborn and Burton were in the Ricky Nelson band and appeared on the Ozzie and Harriet television show each week. Burton would later become a recording icon and spend many years with Elvis Presley, accompanying him on all of his tours and television appearances.

On the way to the studio with Dorsey, we stopped at a small motel to pick up another musician who would play rhythm guitar during the session. When Dorsey introduced me to Glen Campbell I knew immediately who he was. He'd yet to have a hit record, but I had read about him in music magazines. He had been playing in sessions with many of the big stars of the day, including Frank Sinatra. On the long ride to the studio with Dorsey, I was nervous about what I was going to be doing, but that jittery feeling was tempered by the thought of being backed up with a great group of famous musicians, including Glen Campbell, who sat in the backseat as we drove to the studio. It was an opportunity of a lifetime. The union's recording scale for a three-hour session at that time, incidentally, was $65 per person. Can you imagine having that kind of talent available today for that paltry sum?

During the session, the instrument track for all four songs I was to sing was laid down first. It was a wonderful, secure feeling to sit back and listen as this talented group played so flawlessly. The sound was excellent. Everything seemed to come so easy for them as they read their music charts. All four songs were completed in a little over two hours. As they left for other work elsewhere in town, I shook their hands and bid them farewell.

Now it was my turn. There were three women there to sing background. When needed, Dorsey joined in to sing harmony with me. We all wore earphones and sang as we listened to the instrumentation. We completed our work in the allotted three hours and both Dorsey and I were pleased with how the songs turned out.

After the session, Dorsey had to pick something up at the studio where the Ozzie and Harriet television shows were taped. We pulled into a parking lot in the back of the building marked "private." Along the wall were four especially wide parking slots with signs for "Ozzie" "Harriet," "David," and "Ricky." A vehicle was parked in the "Ozzie" slot. The rest were empty. We found Ozzie alone at work, editing the show that was to be aired that week. Dorsey introduced me and it was a very special time for me. I had grown up watching the Ozzie and Harriet television show on KELO. I don't think I missed one episode. Now, here I was, a greenhorn kid from nowhere, meeting Ozzie Nelson, the producer of the show, in the very studio where the episodes were made.

Of the four songs that I recorded, Dorsey selected two, "Town Girl," and "School's Out," and was able to place them on the Delfi Label. The record was released three months later. It received a good rating in *Billboard Magazine* and it was played on many radio stations. But it didn't quite make it. I was crushed, although Dorsey still remained positive about my singing future. He told me that it was only a matter of time before one of my records made it big.

A year after that session, I returned for another recording session at the famous United Studio in Hollywood. The end result was much the same. Looking back now, so many years later, I realize that the odds are against every aspiring singer who hopes to make it big in the music business. At that time, about eight hundred records were produced each week, so radio station program directors across the nation had a plethora of songs from which to pick. My records had good ratings from *Billboard* and *Cash Box Magazine*, but as in any business, everything must mesh and fall into just the right place at the right time.

In the music business, it seems that once that first big hit is realized, the others come much easier for the artist. I confess that during my early career, I always had confidence and felt that my big opportunity was in the next song that came along. I believed that sooner or later, my time would come, and everyone I worked with in the business also thought it was just a matter of time. But as we say in South Dakota, close counts only in horseshoes and hand grenades.

7

Bobby Vee Opens Doors

One of the best things that happened in my life out on the rock and roll circuit was the friendship that formed between Bobby Vee and me. Bobby, born Bobby Velline April 30, 1943, in Fargo, ND, was and is a rock and roll icon. We first met at a popular Moorhead pizza house where all of the musicians gathered after playing their gigs on Saturday nights in the Fargo area.

His big chance came in early February of 1959 when he was just fifteen. After news reached the Fargo-Moorhead area on Feb. 3, 1959, a call went out for local talent to fill in at the event that was to feature Buddy Holly, Ritchie Valens, and The Big Bopper, who had perished that fateful morning in an airplane crash as their plane took off in the snow from Mason City, IA. Bobby and his group, The Shadows, answered the call. He went on to become a teenage idol in the 1960s with a number of chart-topping songs and a variety of albums. He was described by *Billboard Magazine* as "one of the ten most consistent chartmakers ever."

Bobby and his band, The Shadows, had recorded at K-Bank Studios in Minneapolis. He had a regional hit, "Susie Baby." With that popular launching, he soon hit the musical jackpot. "Susie Baby" was picked up by Liberty Records, which was a major label in Los Angeles. The company signed Bobby to a contract and it wasn't long before he was recording hit after hit. He got so big that he soon moved from his home in Fargo, ND, to Los Angeles to be nearer to the recording studio. During his long career (he is still performing), Bobby had thirty-eight top one hundred hits and six gold records. Over thirty million Bobby Vee records have been sold.

Our paths crossed often when we played around the Fargo area and we became close friends. Bobby always told me how much he appreciated the great musicians I had in the band. In the spring of 1963, he called and offered us an opportunity to be his back up band on his upcoming summer tour. He explained that his

This is the newspaper advertisement from Berlin, WI, where Bobby Vee and Myron Lee and the Caddies were scheduled on July 10, 1964. Note the incorrect spelling of "Bobby."

regular band had opted to remain in the Fargo area because of college commitments of some of the members, and for other reasons. Also, Bobby's need for a full-time band was waning so his needs were sporadic. That was because many of his appearances were now promotional in nature and he could lip-sync his songs. He'd fly into a city, do his interviews, hand shaking, visiting, and lip-syncing, and then fly back out again within hours.

It was common for many of the top recording artists then to play dates all over the country using a different pick-up band in each city they visited. It must have been a hassle for them to always be rehearsing with a different band, but it made good business sense to do it that way, rather than take a band along with them. Bobby Vee had a different procedure because he was very particular about his shows and he wanted everything to be well rehearsed so he could give his fans the very best, and you can't fault him for that.

Needless to say, I was happy to accept his offer. Before the tour weighed anchor that July in Harbor Springs, MI, we rehearsed with him for a couple of days. Bobby and I hit it off right away. We were about the same age and were both Dakotans to the core. His records were topping the charts at the time, playing on radio stations all over the world. He had also appeared on all of the big television shows, such as *American Bandstand* and the *Art Linkletter Show* and others. I was happy for him and I envied his success. I hoped that my time would eventually come, as his had, with one big hit to set the banquet table for a string of top forty songs to follow.

On the 1963 tour, as with nearly all tours, each night was basically a mirror image of the night before. The dances would be planned to last about three or four hours. The Caddies would play the dance music. Then Bobby would come out for the standard two, forty-five minute shows, singing such hits as "Take Good Care of My Baby," and "Rubber Ball," both million sellers, plus others such as "Devil or Angel," "Run to Him," and "The Night Has a Thousand Eyes." Of course, he also sang dozens of others that I and his thousands of other fans loved. Whenever possible, Bobby would have us rehearsing something new so that he could keep his show fresh and fun, not only for the audience, but for all of us, too.

Here is Fargo, ND, resident Bobby Vee, carrying his clothing from the Caravan of Stars bus. He was a headliner on the Dick Clark Caravan of Stars in 1963. Bobby and Myron became close friends and it was Bobby who recommended Myron Lee and the Caddies to Clark.

The crowds were unbelievable wherever we played. It was also a joy to be associated with such a big star and all-around nice guy. I usually didn't travel with him, but we were part of his "caravan." He drove an Oldsmobile station wagon and his brother Bill—who was also his road manager and if need be, his bodyguard—rode with him. We followed in my station wagon. Our equipment trailer brought up the rear. That summer was spent mostly on the East Coast, although we did return to the Midwest a couple of times, and were able to enjoy a few days in Sioux Falls with our friends and families. By this time, drummer Chico Hajek had moved on and Marc Rowe from Fargo took over on drums. Marc was not only a drummer, but a great comedian as well. He kept us laughing day and night on those long trips.

We worked eastern seaside resorts from Maine to Florida. The dates on that 1963 tour were spaced so we would have to drive anywhere from one hundred to three hundred miles a day. But a few trips were longer than that. One man-killer was the drive after we played a fair in Regina, Canada, down to the Pennsylvania State Fair. It took us two days. Touring is a grueling, repetitive journey, but I can't think of a time during the entire trip when we weren't enjoying ourselves and just having a barrel of fun.

On a tour of that length there are many times when you don't even know what town you are in. Sometimes, you don't even know what day of the week it is. But I do distinctly remember one part of our tour on a hot summer's night in Montgomery, AL. We'd driven all day in an Alabama oven of 100-degree heat. Finally in Montgomery, we pulled our little convoy into the humongous parking lot surrounding the auditorium where we were booked for the evening. We arrived about 4 p.m., so we had time to kill. We pulled slowly around the building to the back unloading dock. As we did, we noticed that the sides of the auditorium displayed signs the size of boxcars advertising that evening's billing. In addition to Bobby Vee, there were three other acts: Jerry Lee Lewis, Frankie Valle and the Four Seasons, and Roy Orbison. What a billing!

We spotted a snazzy looking, mother of all motor homes parked in the back of the lot under a large shade tree. It was the biggest RV that I'd ever seen. Bobby Vee told us that it belonged to Roy Orbison. Our mouths dropped and our eyes widened with that news. Our eyes opened even larger when Bobby, who had previously worked with Roy, asked us if we'd like to drive over and meet Roy.

Age is catching up with old pals Myron and Bobby Vee, at Bobby Vee's concert in the late 1990s at the Ramkota in Sioux Falls.

66

We pulled up in front of the motor home and Bobby knocked on the door. Roy answered. He seemed glad to see us, and with a sweep of his hand, invited us in. The home's air conditioning did its part contributing to a memorable, comfortable couple of hours. Roy and his wife were the perfect hosts and kept the cold beer coming, along with snacks and repartee. I must say that I've never enjoyed a beer more, unless it was in the poolhall back in Parker when I was ten.

That evening, Jerry Lee Lewis opened the show with his trademark, helter-skelter, forty-five minutes of excitement. Then Frankie Valle and the Four Seasons came out to loud applause. We kids from Sioux Falls just stood back in the wings enthralled at how well they all sang their litany of hits.

Bobby Vee and The Caddies were the third act and then there was an intermission before Roy Orbison closed out the show. And did he ever close it! As the house lights dimmed for Roy, Bobby beckoned me over to where he was standing and suggested we go out front and find a couple of empty seats in the back of the auditorium. "Have you ever seen Orbison in person?" he asked as we walked to the front hall to enter the auditorium. I told him I hadn't. "Well," he said, "then you just gotta see this." A helpful usher found a couple of empty seats somewhat away from the rest of the crowd, far in the back where Bobby wouldn't be easily recognized—and mobbed. Roy sauntered out on stage wearing his trademark dark glasses. The crowd of about 20,000 cheered, and then it was silent as he began to sing one hit after another of the songs he had written.

What a talent. The songs of his were so well known to everyone that many in the crowd silently mouthed the words as Roy sang. I knew all the words, too. There was "Only the Lonely," "Dream Baby," Blue Bayou," "Running Scared," "Crying," "Candyman," "In Dreams," and on and on. After a wonderful forty-five minutes that seemed like five or ten, he closed his show with "Pretty Woman." People jumped to their feet calling for more. I must confess that I'd never seen such a magic affinity between a performer and an audience. Roy started to leave the stage, and the urgings of the crowd grew even louder. "More, More," they chanted in unison, and Bobby and I joined in. Roy returned to center stage and performed not one encore, but three. Then, with a polite bow and a wave, he was gone. The crowd was still abuzz and smiling as they began to leave the auditorium. I turned to Bobby and asked him if it was always like that when Roy performed. "You bet," he said. "I've worked with him several times and it's always exactly like this. People just love his music." It was a memorable experience for me, and probably for everyone there.

Even today, forty years after that Montgomery show, I have yet to see or hear anything like that Orbison appearance. Now, long after his death on Dec. 6, 1988, in Henderson, TN, of a massive heart attack, his songs and his voice live on. I'm blessed to have been among those privileged to have met him and heard him sing.

As our 1963 summer tour was ending, I got the surprise of my life. Bobby nonchalantly mentioned that he'd been signed as the headlining artist for the Caravan of Stars tour being organized by Dick Clark for that fall. It was scheduled to begin in November, with twelve acts on the show's billing. Bobby mentioned Jimmy

Clanton and The Ronnettes of "Be My Baby" fame as two of the other acts in the show.

Then, in an off the cuff manner, Bobby said: "Oh, by the way Myron, would you be interested in being the band to back up this show?" I didn't know what to say. I was overwhelmed. I nearly fainted.

I later learned that Clark had asked Bobby for his recommendation for the tour's band. Bobby told him we would be great. As is the case in so many instances, it is often who you know. Without Bobby's recommendation, there would have been no way in the world that we would have even been considered for what was the best job in America for a rock and roll band. In the next chapter, I'll tell you about the exciting Dick Clark tour.

The next summer, 1964, Bobby asked me if we could make the tour with him again. Of course we could, and it was another enjoyable tour made even more special because of a stop we made in Clovis, NM.

Clovis was the home of Norman Petty, who had been the manager of Buddy Holly. As we were playing on the Clovis High School stage, I happened to glance into the wings. There stood Norman Petty watching us while he moved subtly to the beat of our music. I'd done two recording sessions earlier in my career at his famous recording studio in Clovis, and Bobby had recorded an album there called "Bobby Vee Meets The Crickets." The sight of Petty off to the side must have sent an extra shot of adrenalin through my system, because I noticed that I was really putting all of my heart and soul into playing and singing.

After our show, Petty invited all of us to tour his new recording studio that had just been completed. It had been a life-long dream of his. The studio came with all of the bells and whistles you'd expect to find in a state-of-the-art recording set-up. He'd bought an old, empty movie theater building in downtown Clovis and invested a couple of million dollars converting it into his offices and the recording studio. After the tour, we bid Norman Petty farewell. I left with the renewed impression that he was a man of character and integrity, not to mention talent and knowledge of the business. I was thrilled to have spent time with a man who had done so much for the music industry, and for struggling South Dakota musicians such as ourselves.

Many of the performances on that 1964 tour with Bobby Vee were scheduled closer to home. We even played the Sioux Falls Coliseum. It was very enjoyable for all of us to look out into the audience and see classmates, friends, and neighbors from Sioux Falls and the surrounding area. For a dropout kid with a bad habit of falling asleep in classes at Washington High School, it was gratifying to return to prove to others that while I may not have measured up as a student, I was on stage with Bobby Vee, an international star.

During that 1964 tour we started in May and traveled the East Coast again. We ended our summer odyssey on June 6 at the Texas Teen Fair in San Antonio, TX. It was an excellent stop at just the right time. The fair lasted a week and we performed once each day, so we had a chance to unwind and relax. We didn't have to rush around to prepare for another long and hectic car trip each day. The three-hour show started at 10 a.m. each day. We did a forty-five minute portion.

The morning program started with country singer George Jones and The Jones Boys. I'd been a Jones fan for years. A few years earlier he had recorded my favorite, "She Thinks I Still Care," and it was a big hit. Working with him at the fair, I found him to be two different people, really. Other than his great talent, he made no large impression on me.

After his show each day, as we waited back stage for our part, George would rush past us with his eyes on the stage door and his band scurrying along behind him. He was beckoning back and playfully yelling out in his thick southern accent, "Last Call For Alkie-Hall!" George, who was about thirty years old at the time, loved to drink. Later in his career, his liking for liquor nearly killed him in a very bad car accident caused when he reached down for his bottle of vodka, police said. George had one hit named "If Drinkin Don't Kill Me (Her Memory Will)." It included the line: "With the blood from my body I could start my own still." There was probably some truth to that.

So after his 1964 Texas Teen Fair show each day, he and his entourage headed back to the Holiday Inn where we were also staying. George was an outgoing, personable fellow on stage, but seemed to morph into something of a recluse the rest of the time. He spent hours every day holed up in his motel room. They said he'd drink the day away and then pass out. But he was a pro, that's for sure, because the next morning, he was up with the chickens and ready to entertain. He did his performance to perfection, then rushed to the stage door with his call for "alkie-hall" and settle in at the motel for another day with old John Barleycorn. His talent was immense and we were all big fans and thrilled to be on the same show with him.

After our part in the show each day we went back to the Holiday Inn, too. We spent most afternoons lounging around the swimming pool, getting Texas tans. Jones, who in 1969 would marry Tammy Wynette, was accompanied in Texas by a pretty young lady. I was never sure if they were married or not. She, too, spent afternoons at the pool, while George remained alone back in his room, drinking the day away. His preference to be alone was something similar to that of Bobby Rydell, another Texas Teen Fair performer who also seemed to prefer not to mix with the rest of us.

One day after we'd all consumed a few beers and were lollygagging around the pool and looking for trouble, George's lady friend suggested we all go up and get George to join us. "Let's get that SOB and throw him in the pool," she suggested. We were all for it and set out on our raid. His lady unlocked their motel door and we burst into his room. George wasn't too happy with us and he resisted all the way to the pool. But his "condition" worked in our favor. We'd all assumed that after his dunking in a cool pool, he might relax a bit and join in the fun we were having. We tossed him in, he sank to the bottom, came bubbling back up spouting pool water like a big white whale, swam to a pool ladder, and hoisted himself out without as much as a comment. He failed to see the humor in our delight and he stomped back to his room, mumbling all the way. His behavior that day and on others that followed were different, to say the least. But no one would argue that his credentials as a country singer were anything but impeccable.

Also entertaining Texas teens just before us each day was a little-known group from England called The Rolling Stones. They were on their first North American tour. English music was just beginning to be noticed in this country, and it was catching on like wildfire. At the time, The Rolling Stones hit "I Can't Get No Satisfaction" was at the top of the charts. The Stones then seemed shy and withdrawn around other artists who were back stage. Maybe aloof is a better description. None of them ever had much to say. I thought at the time that possibly they were just uppity Englishmen. But first impressions can be incorrect and mine certainly were. They turned out to be very nice people who at that time didn't want to appear pushy with strangers and were still feeling their way along with American artists.

Years later, in the mid-1990s, our former drummer Stu Perry told me he'd once spent time with Keith Richards, the Stones guitar player. During the conversation, Stu asked Richards if he remembered the Texas Teen show in the early 1960s. He did. Stu asked if he remembered a group called Myron Lee and the Caddies. Richards acknowledged that he certainly did. "Are you kidding me?" Stu asked. "No, of course I remember," Richards replied. "We were thrilled because you guys were the first American band we got to perform with." I've always thought that was one of the nicest compliments one could receive.

Also appearing at the Texas Teen Fair in 1963 was Robert Louis Ridarelli, a.k.a. Bobby Rydell. He closed the show with many of his hits. Throughout the week, and usually everywhere that stars of the day performed on the same stage, it was common for all of us in the show to mill, mess around, and mingle back stage, joking, catching up on music news and, of course, listening to the music of others.

Bobby Rydell, the 21-year-old South Philly kid, avoided all that. He never spent much time with the rest of us. Before his part in the show, he remained outside in his limo parked near the entrance to the dressing rooms. When it was time for him to perform, he marched directly to the stage, right past all of us, without even a nod. His manager was always at his side. I thought the manager, who had that easily recognized East Coast, standoffish attitude, perhaps believed that by appearing aloof, Bobby might acquire some of the persona of Elvis Presley. Tom Parker, who managed Elvis, was known to hold "The King" back, and discouraged his mixing with his peers. We never got to know the real Bobby Ridarelli during the Teen Fair. We only worked with a great singer known as Bobby Rydell.

8

Dick Clark's Caravan of Stars

The Caravan of Stars tour in 1963 was one of the biggest breaks in my career.

There I was, a struggling musician born in Parker, South Dakota, with plenty of Sioux Falls dust on my boots, being invited to be a part of the most prestigious tour of the day by none other than Dick Clark of ABC's *American Bandstand*.

I have Bobby Vee to thank for the opportunity. He told Clark about us, and convinced him that we could handle the job of playing backup for all of the singers signed on for the caravan.

Clark was the Babe Ruth and the Mickey Mantle of the rock and roll music business and the music world in general. He could recognize talent and a potential hit song and turn a single record into a home run. To youngsters, Dick Clark was almost magic. He was the idol of millions then, and still is. He has an eye and an ear for good music and for decades has had a tremendous influence on popular music. If he hears something he believes has potential, and plays it on his radio or television show, everyone in the industry picks up on it and plays it, too. Every young singer in the country hoped and dreamed of being noticed by Dick Clark.

Bobby told me that Clark had suggested that it would be best if I added two more musicians to the band. He thought the newcomers should be horn players. That would grow our little group to a seven-piece band. I wasn't too enamored with a seven-piece band, and mentioned my concern. As we rolled along through eastern Minnesota on the last leg of our 1963 tour, Bobby told me the Clark Caravan would start in New York City. A contingent of about sixty people would travel on two buses, and would perform mostly one-night stands for four to five weeks, traveling throughout the United States.

My unlikely response to Clark's invitation, delivered through Bobby, was to ask Bobby if he thought the band could handle such a big responsibility. There must have been hundreds of bands like ours in the nation just waiting for a chance like what we had been offered. Bobby said he had "no doubt" that we would be perfect. He added that was exactly what he told Dick Clark, too. But always the conservative South Dakotan, I asked Bobby to give me a few days to think it over. Was I crazy, or what?

I wanted to talk to the guys in my band to see how each member felt about it. And I felt obliged to talk to Carole, too. We'd been married on June 26, 1963. Since we were now a partnership, and were also expecting a baby in December, it seemed only fair to discuss the possibility of my being gone for two months, possibly including Christmas. If I accepted Clark's offer, who knows where I would be on the day Carole needed to go to the hospital.

The band members were gung ho about the tour and were ready to go. Carole was, too, and I am forever grateful to her for that. When we talked about it, she was more excited about the opportunity for me than I was. She encouraged me to take it and run. I called Bobby. "Let's do it," I told him. We would soon be off on one of the most exciting, rewarding experiences of my life.

In 1963, Fred Scott, our sax man, was drafted into the Army. When he was back in Sioux Falls on leave after a few weeks of basic training, I shared with him the good news about the new job coming up with the Dick Clark tour. Fred was a consummate musician who had worked hard to reach the top of his profession. Naturally, he was very disappointed that he couldn't go along because of his military commitment. We would miss him. He was such a great musician and also a good friend of mine. It would be difficult to find a suitable replacement.

As his time to leave Sioux Falls and return to duty approached, Fred decided that he simply would not report back. He was determined to take his lumps with the Army, and perhaps then could return to his chosen and much-loved profession. He wanted desperately to accompany us on the Clark caravan. So he hatched a plan for him to "accidentally" shoot himself in the foot with his .22 caliber rifle. Jerry Haacke, Fred, and I drove out to the dump ground west of Sioux Falls ostensibly to hunt rats. It was a Saturday morning and no one was around. I'll let Fred tell you in his own words what transpired there:

"We walked around for a little bit at the dump and then I decided that I just couldn't shoot myself in the foot. We were walking back to Jerry's car when the gun went off. I don't know. Was it an accident or not? I really don't know. Anyway, it got me in the foot. We got to the hospital and they took care of the wound. It really didn't hurt that much, but the doctors told me that I was lucky because the bullet didn't do any serious damage.

"They put my foot in a cast. I knew right from the start that I wasn't going to try to hide from authorities or to avoid a confrontation with the Army if they came to get me. So I stayed around Sioux Falls until they picked me up. When they got me to Ft. Leavenworth they processed me like everyone they had picked up over the weekend. The first thing was that they asked everyone there if they wanted to return to duty. That particular Monday morning there were about forty of us in the room.

All of the others said yes, except me. Those that said yes were processed and sent back to their units. I had to talk to the captain in charge, who seemed sympathetic to my cause. I told him about the Dick Clark tour and that it was the big opportunity I had worked all my life to achieve and he nodded understandingly. To make a long story short, I eventually visited a psychiatrist and a judge advocate general who turned red as a beet as I gave him my reasons, and, in a veritable snit, dismissed me from his office. But later, I received a General Discharge Under Honorable Conditions, given 'for the good of the service' and therefore, I received all of the rights and privileges of an honorable discharge."

That was Fred's story. Of course, I had no idea of what was going on in his life as he recuperated from his wound and dealt with authorities at Ft. Leavenworth. We were scheduled to leave for the tour in a week and I still hadn't found a replacement for him. I was desperate and called Clark's manager to explain my predicament. He didn't seem to be too concerned, and told me not to worry. We could find a suitable horn man from the local musicians union in New York. I would much rather have had someone I knew as part of our band, but this was an emergency. I gradually accepted the fact that we would be traveling on the tour with a New York union musician.

Fortunately, early on the morning that we were about to head east for New York, I received a call from Fred. He said the Army had decided to let him go, and he inquired if I'd filled the horn spot. I hadn't, of course, and Fred was ecstatic. We didn't have time to wait for him to get back to Sioux Falls from St. Louis, so I arranged for him to fly to New York to meet us there.

But before all of this, long before we left Sioux Falls, and before Fred's foot wound, the mailman dropped off a thick envelope containing my contract with Clark. Included in the fine print was a clause dealing with my preference to add just one horn player rather than two. Happily, the contract called for The Caddies to be a six-member band. That's what I had hoped for, and my rationale wasn't completely related to music. It also had to do with the logistics of getting from Sioux Falls to New York City in my station wagon. The long trip would be much easier and more comfortable for six band members, as opposed to seven.

The contract also spelled out the pay. I would receive a check each week for $1,200. From that, I had to pay the salaries of each of the five other musicians. Dick Clark would provide transportation once we arrived in New York City, and he would also provide motel or hotel rooms for all of us during the tour. Each band member would be responsible for other expenses, such as their incidentals and meals.

Several weeks before the tour was to start, I received a list of the artists who would appear on the show. Because we were to provide the music for all of the performers, I felt it was important that we begin rehearsing right away. We wanted to be ready before we got to New York City because after the tour started, there would be precious little time to be working out musical details. We spent several hours every day rehearsing in my makeshift "rehearsal hall." It was in an apartment house I bought when I turned twenty-one. The apartment was on Eighth and Summit. For a time, Carole and I lived free in a basement apartment. The rent income from the other three units made our house payments.

When the largest apartment in the complex became empty, I didn't rent it so it could be used for our rehearsals. I purchased all of the records of the Caravan of Stars artists I could find. We listened to the records, then memorized our part for each song with no problem. The musicians in my band were all excellent at what they did. Interestingly, the only two who could read music were Fred Scott and Joel Shapiro, the saxophone players. The rest of us could only read charts. This was not necessarily a hindrance, however. I

This cover letter came to Myron in 1963 with the contracts for his band's part in the Dick Clark Caravan of Stars.

remember one time when Johnny Carson asked the great guitar player Chet Atkins if he knew how to read music. Chet replied: "I read a little, but not enough to hurt my playing."

Curt Powell handled the lead guitar, Jerry Haacke was on bass, and Stu Perry was on drums. I was the band leader, singer, and played rhythm guitar. We were a team of six, and, I felt, pretty good at what we did.

During the pre-tour rehearsals, we concentrated on the songs of everyone who would be on the tour except Bobby Vee, who would be the headliner. By this time we'd worked with Bobby so often that we knew his music and his routine. The other stars that we would be backing up would be Brian Hyland, Linda Scott, Jimmy Clanton, The Essex, The Jaynettes, The Ronnettes, Little Eva, The Dixie Belles, Dale and Grace, Joe Perkins, Donald Jenkins and the Delighters, The Dovelles, Paul and Paula, The Tymes, and Jeff Condon. All of them had hit records on the charts and we were honored to have been invited to be a part of such a great show.

The fall weather in Sioux Falls was great and our "rehearsal hall" windows were still open as we worked our way through all of the music we would be required to play on the tour. Neighbors, much to our surprise, were not only forgiving of our musical intrusions, but often dropped by to listen.

Jimmy Thomas, our booking agent, seemed happy for us and for the opportunity, but he wasn't exactly enamored that we would be gone and not available for listings on his booking ledger for much of the remainder of 1963. But promoter that he was, he knew that in the long run, the tour would be a feather in our hats and would help him in his booking of us for future jobs.

The day arrived for our departure and we packed our instruments and clothing sufficient to fit into one suitcase each into our faithful trailer. November 6, 1963, dawned bright and clear. Carole and I said our goodbyes and we were off on the biggest adventure of our young lives.

As we pulled away in my new 1963 red Ford Country Squire station wagon, I glanced back in the rear-view and saw Carole, growing each day into her maternity clothes, waving goodbye. We'd all been so nervous getting ready to leave that morning that we hadn't eaten breakfast. I stopped at the McDonald's on East Eighth Street and ordered some of their fifteen-cent burgers to go. At that time, the Interstate Highway was mainly lines of ribbon-bedecked survey stakes. So until we got to Chicago, the roads were mostly two-lane through every small town. Once we were rolling, we never stopped except to take on gas and food. We shared the driving and went straight through to our eastern rendezvous.

We were blessed by the weather all of the way. When the odometer racked up near the 1,400-mile mark, we could see the skyline of New York ahead. Somehow, perhaps it was dumb luck, we successfully navigated through a myriad of streets and highways to the Sheraton Park Hotel on Seventh Avenue and Fifty-Sixth Street, where we all were to meet the next day. I rented a storage room at the hotel for our equipment and instruments. Clark's tour manager had already made arrangements to have my car and trailer stored away while we would be gone. I paid a $250 storage fee to an unfriendly, surly worker there, and as I walked away, I wondered if I would ever see my car or trailer again.

We checked into the hotel rooms that had been reserved for us. I gave Carole a call to tell her we'd all arrived safe and sound, then checked in with Clark's road manager to let him know we were there.

After getting settled, in predictable hicks-from-the-sticks fashion, we then hailed a taxi and told the driver to take us to Times Square. We strained our necks and gawked and adjusted to the city's "verticalness," after a lifetime in our flatland, horizontal world. We then had dinner before heading back to our hotel for a good night's sleep before the big day ahead. The next morning at 8 a.m., everyone on the tour was to be in the hotel lobby to board buses to our rehearsal site.

We reported to our assigned blue and white Greyhound bus Number One with "Caravan of Stars" emblazoned on the sides. It would be our home away from home for the next thirty days. A twin to our bus was parked behind ours, rumbling with diesel and ready to go. In all, counting the singing groups and others, there would be sixty people on the tour. I recognized many of the stars with whom we would be working, having seen many on Clark's television show. I thought I had died and gone to heaven, rubbing shoulders and sharing a bus, as we were, with some of the nation's rock and roll greats.

Our first bus ride was brief. We rode over the river, escorted by the ubiquitous darting yellow New York taxies, to Teaneck, NJ, where we would rehearse for the first time before our premier performance there that evening. Our bus pulled in behind the 8,000-seat Teaneck Auditorium, the bus brakes hissed, the folding door slapped open, and things were about to become even more fun and exciting for us.

We began setting up our band equipment. Clark's officious road manager, Ed McAdams, a retired Marine that everyone called Sarge, marched up and handed me the sheet of paper with the order of performances. Sarge had a gruff, drill sergeant demeanor, but as the tour progressed, we got to know him and he turned out to be a puppy dog and a very nice man.

Ed McAdams was known affectionately as "Sarge" during the Dick Clark Caravan of Stars bus tours. As Clark's road manager, he made the arrangements and then, over the bus speaker system, advised those on the caravan when and where to be at any specific time.

We started that first rehearsal with Jimmy Clanton, who would open the show in the evening. He had five songs. I nervously thumbed through my notebook to his name so I could make notes on his preferences and to jot down comments on each song. I had earlier noted the key in which each song was to be played. All of the other stars were lounging out in the front seats of the auditorium to watch and listen and pass the time away.

It was my responsibility to tell my band the name of each song as it came up and to count off the proper tempo. Considering that we were up there in the spotlight while the veterans and experts were out there critiquing us from the first few rows waiting their turns, we did just great. The practice sessions back in Sioux Falls had prepared us well. Five hours and about sixty songs later we were done. It was about 6 p.m. We headed to the dressing room to relax a bit and to change and prepare for the show that would start at 7 p.m. Walking into the dressing room filled with famous performers was intimidating, to say the least. I was this shy guy from South Dakota, and I wondered for a moment what in the world I had gotten myself into. Many of the performers knew one another from working on previous shows. It seemed for a few moments as if we were imposing on a fraternity party to which we hadn't been invited. But it wasn't too many shows later that we were accepted into the group and we soon joined in the fun, too.

A short time later Clark walked in. The noise quickly subsided. Clark hadn't been on the buses on the ride over from New York, so this was the first time we Caddies had seen him in person. He greeted some of his old friends who had appeared on his television show, shook some hands, nodded and waved to people, and eventually made his way over to me. He smiled and reached out to shake my hand.

"Hi—I'm Dick Clark," he said with a smile.

Naturally, I knew that anyway, but he was kind and courteous and he made me feel as if I were part of the group. He asked me how I was doing. I told him that I was slightly nervous and worried that we'd be able to do our part well.

"Myron," he said, "I've felt like that myself many times, and believe me, it might be a little rough at first, but the audience won't even notice."

He said that Bobby Vee had told him about us, and he had every confidence. "Your band is great and I have no doubt that everything is going to be just fine." He told me to "just relax and do what you do. I'll guarantee you that by the time we do the fourth show in four days, everything will fall into place and you will look back and laugh at how you're feeling right now."

I was twenty-two years old at that time. Dick Clark was thirty-three. He was so down-to-earth, very professional, and charismatic. He had a calming effect on me, and on the rest of the band. After his pep talk, I was ready to walk

Dick Clark, backstage during the 1963 Caravan of Stars tour, makes an adjustment on something or other using the auditorium's work bench vice.

through the brick wall to get up to the stage and get started. So were the other band members. But reason prevailed and we took the usual route to the stage. The place was packed. The plan was for us to begin the evening with one high-energy song to get things started with a bang while people just arriving had time to find their seats.

Our song ended, and then it was my job to get the show underway. I wasn't provided a script, but each night it was my job to introduce Dick Clark.

"Good evening everyone," I'd say. "Now—direct from *American Bandstand*—Dick Clark."

Some nights I would change the intro around somewhat, and perhaps add something about the city in which we were performing. After I introduced him with a sweep of my arm to the wings where he was waiting, he walked out on the stage to the cheers of the crowd. People in the audience went absolutely bonkers each evening. It was clear then that he had this special gift of stage presence. He was in control. The audience responded to all that he said and to each gesture he made.

It was a rush for me each time I introduced him, night after night, in places like Johnstown, PA, Davenport, IA, St. Louis, or Pittsburgh. Every time he came out, his comments varied with the time and the place. It was different every night, designed to personalize and fit the city and the events of the day. Serving as the master of ceremony and the hub of the evening's performance was just part of his responsibilities on the caravan. Every day in every city, he made himself available to the media for comments and questions. He had an insatiable appetite for work.

Incidentally, we were in Scranton, PA, on our fourth night for the fourth show. Clark's reassurances after our rehearsal in Teaneck proved to be correct. As I stood on stage on that fourth night, I was relaxed and in control and I thought the band sounded perfect, just as he said it would. We were all having the time of our lives. I thought back to that first night in Teaneck when I was tense as a guitar string, worried about how we might do. Clark had it right all along.

Even today, so many years later, people who remember the tour ask me how Dick Clark was to work with. I tell them about Elkhart, Indiana. Incidentally, an old high school classmate then attending Notre Dame came to our Elkhart performance. Dennis McFarland, who is now a successful attorney in Sioux Falls, was a welcome face in the very big crowd.

We did a rare daytime show for Dennis McFarland and the others in Elkhart, so we were free that evening. Clark had arranged a night-off party for all of us. There was music, food, and plenty of refreshments. The day before the party, slips of paper with the names of all of the performers were dropped in a hat. Each person or act then drew out a name and had to sing one of the songs that the act had in the show. We set up the band as we did for every regular show, and accompanied each singer. As I remember it, the off-the-cuff show started out something like this:

Freddie Cannon drew out Dick Clark's name, and our private show started with me introducing Freddie as I always did for Clark. He became the master of ceremonies. Bobby Vee drew Freddie Cannon's name and sang one of his songs, which happened to be "Way Down Yonder In New Orleans." Dick Clark drew Little Eva's name. He wore a dress to the party similar to one that Little Eva might wear, and he sang her hit, "The Locomotion." On and on the performance went, with everyone hamming it up. It was hilarious.

I think Clark and Sarge had ordered every variety of liquid refreshment known to man. The buffet seemed as long as Philips Avenue back home in Sioux Falls. As the evening progressed, and the refreshments continued to flow, a food fight developed. Someone, I don't remember who it was, dumped a bowl of potato salad on another star's head. By about 1 a.m., things had calmed down and people started drifting back to their rooms. The band and I began to tear down the equipment and carry it back to the bus for next morning's 8 a.m. departure. The only person who remained behind to help us was Dick Clark. He grabbed what he could and helped us haul it all out to the elevator and then onto the buses. He didn't stop until we were finished. He's a millionaire, yet he pitched in like a

This 1963 picture was taken during the Dick Clark Caravan of Stars tour of the East Coast. From left to right, Dick Clark, Jerry Haacke, Joel Shapiro, Myron Lee, Fred Scott, Curt Powell, and drummer Stu Perry.

member of the band. That impressed me. I decided that deep down, despite his fame and fortune, he was one of us.

Clark always rode on the bus with us. Once on an all-night ride, the bus slowed going through a little town. Clark spotted a small cafe that was open in the wee hours of the morning. He told the driver to pull over. We all piled out and all sixty of us went in for breakfast. There were just two people on duty. Both seemed shocked until they recognized Clark and some of the stars.

Clark told them about the tour and offered our services to help in preparing breakfasts for the sixty people now in that the small cafe. Some of us became waiters and waitresses. Clark volunteered to fry the eggs. Brian Hyland was put in charge of bacon frying. Bobby Vee, well known as a pancake aficionado, volunteered for that task. It was one of the most enjoyable early-morning breakfasts I can remember. The camaraderie that developed that morning brought us all even closer together for the long haul ahead.

Another time, we stopped at a little, out-of-the-way grocery store in a small town in the east somewhere and practically cleaned it out of snacks, candy bars, and other munchies. Someone bought wine and cheese. We ate and drank and toasted through the night as the buses rumbled down the highway to our next show, but there was no over indulgence, and there never was during all of the tour, except for our private party in Elkhart.

Dick Clark, who wore his laurels lightly, could have traveled from show to show in a limo or flown on a chartered airplane. But he preferred—and it was obvious that he thoroughly enjoyed—being "one of the gang." He was with us for much of the tour, except on weekends when he flew back to Philadelphia to do his television show. Then he'd fly back to our next stop and the following morning climb back on board the bus again. He enjoyed playing cribbage. Sometimes, the games continued for hours and hours as our bus carried through the night to the next date. Our sax man, Fred Scott, loosened the shoe laces on his still-healing foot and settled in up front as one of the regular cribbage challengers.

When you're locked up in a bus on long trips, you get to know your fellow travelers very well. Sleep was a favorite bus pastime, but we also spent time visiting and playing practical jokes on one another. There were often impromptu sing-alongs. Brian Hyland always had his guitar handy. He was a devil-may-care, laid back kid of about eighteen who had huge hits beginning with "Itsy Bitsy Teenie Weenie Yellow Polka Dot Bikini," and the beautiful hit ballad "Sealed With a Kiss." He helped liven up our sing-alongs and he had a quick wit and ready smile. He liked to hang around with the band, perhaps because we were all about the same age. I often thought that he probably would have been just as happy to be one of the band members making a few hundred dollars a week, rather than the thousands his songs were making for him. Brian is still in the business and still doing very well.

Our tour hopscotched along the East Coast with a few forays out into the Midwest, and we looked forward to performing nearer our home state of South Dakota. The closest we got to Sioux Falls was the performance in Sioux City, IA, on Nov. 20, 1963.

The audience in the big Sioux City Auditorium seemed to be filled with familiar faces that we'd seen many times before when we played dances and other events in the area. And of course, friends and family members of our band were there, too. Carole, now eight months pregnant, came down with bass man Jerry Haacke's girlfriend Shirley. We'd only been gone for two weeks, but the night was especially memorable because we got to play for all of our fans in the Sioux City area.

After the show, we were able to spend some time with our families at a local restaurant before we had to hop back on the bus and headed to Wichita. After the Wichita show, we were bus-bound again for Dallas, TX, where a sad chapter in American history was about to be written.

9

Another Clark Tour and a Death in Dallas

The Caravan of Stars arrived in Dallas on Nov. 22, 1963. It was 10 in the morning when the buses pulled up to the Hilton Hotel in downtown Dallas. The plan was to get some sleep and then board the buses at 5 p.m. for the ride to Memorial Auditorium where the sold-out show was to start at 8 p.m. Fred Scott and I were sharing a room. As we were settling in, we heard on television that President John F. Kennedy would arrive in the city in a few minutes. The president's motorcade route was announced. It would pass by a few blocks from the Hilton. To heck with sleep, I decided, let's go down and watch the motorcade pass by. Fred begged off, saying he was too tired, probably from too much all-night cribbage with Clark on the trip down. So I called Brian Hyland in the room next door. He was happy to go along.

It was a beautiful morning. Brian and I found a good spot on the motorcade route. Within minutes, the crowd had grown four and five deep behind us. Along the planned route for as far as we could see either way were the curious and well-wishers. Soon, right in front of us, was the big black convertible with the President and Jackie in the back seat. Both were waving, smiling, and nodding to the crowd. Attentive secret service men trotted along on either side of the vehicle, scanning the parade route for any suspicious activity. Texas Gov. John Connelly and his wife waved from the convertible's front seat. I still remember how surprised I was by President Kennedy's hair. It was so thick and neat, every strand exactly in place. He was a handsome guy. It was a little like watching royalty pass by. We waved to him and he looked our way and waved back. I thought that he had surely picked us out of that welcoming crowd for that special greeting. The car passed within twenty-five feet of us, and then it was gone.

After the president's car passed, I glanced to my left and noticed a large Nieman Marcus store sign about a half-block away. It was the flagship store of the famous chain was started in Dallas in the early 1900s. I'd heard of its ritzy clothing and other things. It was a unique store that I just had to see. As Brian and I walked to the store three or four minutes after the president's cavalcade had passed, we heard what we thought were firecrackers. That would be a normal part of the downtown celebration that day, I thought. I never dreamed that it might be gunfire.

Inside the store, we paused at a counter. I could see a black and white television set nearby. Then I heard the lady behind the counter near the set say "Oh, no!" I looked at her stunned face that was staring at the television set. My eyes went to the screen, too, and there was a bulletin, and then the announcer came on and said that shots had been fired at the President's motorcade. He said that early reports indicated the President had been hit.

Others in the store gathered around and we all watched in stunned silence. Walter Cronkite at CBS network headquarters came on and confirmed what had happened. The President was dead, he said, fighting back tears. He had been shot once in the head and once in the throat. Then I remembered the sound of firecrackers. It was later determined that those sounds came from the Texas Book Depository a few blocks from where we stood listening to the terrible news brought to us by Walter Cronkite. A sick feeling came over me. I turned to Brian and suggested we get back to the hotel. Sirens were sounding everywhere, it seemed, and they continued to echo through the concrete canyons of Dallas all through the day and night. Entering the Hilton, I noticed that the hotel clerk was crying. We went to our rooms. I flopped down on the bed and turned on the television set. I called Carole. She told me she had also heard the news and had been worried about me.

Later that afternoon, a poignant scene appeared in the Dallas sky, framed in my hotel window. On the television screen, we watched as Air Force One took off with Vice-President Lyndon Johnson, Mrs. Kennedy, and other important government officials on board, as well as the body of the slain president. I glanced from the television screen over to my hotel window and could see the scene in real time. The aircraft banked and headed toward the nation's Capitol.

We soon got a call to tell us that the evening concert in Dallas had been cancelled. Our show the next day in Oklahoma City had also been scratched. So the next morning, we all filed silently out to the bus for a ride to St. Louis and a Nov. 24 engagement in the famous Keil Auditorium. As I was checking into the hotel in St. Louis, as if the shock of the President's assignation hadn't been enough, I looked over to a television set just as Jack Ruby was walking up to the heavily guarded Lee Harvey Oswald, the president's assassin, shooting Oswald at close range.

Not surprisingly, the St. Louis show that night lacked the usual pizzazz, excitement, and joyous fans. The crowd was small. I don't believe any American, including those of us with the Caravan of Stars, was in the mood for entertainment. It was instead a time of mourning and reflection. Clark told the audience in his introductory comments that we all shared a deep sadness, but that we couldn't stop living. He said we all needed to go on.

"We're here tonight," I remember him saying, "and we hope we can put a little joy into your life."

We were supposed to play in Nashville the following evening, Nov. 25. I looked forward to performing in the historic and famous "Music City USA" and seeing Beale Street in the entertainment district. But that date, too, was cancelled because of the president's funeral as the nation continued to mourn.

Our tour limped along in anti-climactic fashion until it ended on Dec. 8. But from then on, the crowds everywhere were much smaller and the people more subdued. The tour ended back in New York City where it had started. I walked to the storage garage, dreading another meeting with the discourteous worker. He hadn't changed, but I was surprised that both the car and trailer were there as I had left them, covered with a thin layer of New York dust that vehicular idleness had encouraged.

As a final gesture, Clark dropped by and personally thanked all of us for our part in the tour. He handed each member of the band a new $100 bill and a nice "thank you" note. As the band leader, he handed me two $100 bills. The Caddies bid farewell to New York City and headed west. We had foul weather for most of the trip back to good old South Dakota. The tour had been an historic, demanding, hectic, excitement-filled journey, and now it was difficult to make the adjustment to the slower pace. Jimmy Thomas, our booking agent, had been busy in our absence. He had us booked for a Luverne, MN, engagement a few days after we got back.

The rest of that winter of 1963 was a rerun of what we'd been doing before we left, playing dates that Jimmy arranged. It was different to go out and play ballrooms again, greeted by a few hundred people after we'd been immersed in the big time with thousands of screaming fans out beyond the bright lights. But it was good to be back home.

Our job on the night of Dec. 23, 1963, was especially memorable for me. We were playing a Christmas party in Jasper, MN. About 10 p.m., I was handed a note.

"Call home immediately."

I suspected what was happening, so I took a break, found a phone, and called Carole. I caught her just as she was leaving with a neighbor, who would drive her to Sioux Valley Hospital. The baby's time had come. Our conversation was brief. I told her that I'd be there just as soon as humanly possible. In those days, out on the road, your work hours were spelled out by contract. That night's contract stipulated that we were to play

Myron is at left and Curt Powell in the center as the The Caddies provide the music for Billy Stewart during the 1963 Caravan of Stars tour. Here they are playing in a high school gymnasium in Bluefield, West Virginia.

until 1 a.m. on Christmas Eve day. The hour of 1 a.m. arrived and we broke down our equipment and packed it away in the trailer in record time. We drove through snow and ice to Sioux Falls thirty miles away. I got to Carole's room about 2:30 a.m. to learn that I was the father of an eight pound baby boy who had came into the world just before midnight. We named him Bobby V. Wachendorf. The middle initial was in honor of my good friend, Bobby Vee, with whom I had worked so many times and who had opened so many doors for me.

As I held my newborn son, I thought of my dad and imagined that he had held me and experienced the same feelings that I was experiencing. It was a happy moment in my life.

Carole was naturally somewhat disappointed that I had been absent when Bobby was born. But she was very understanding of

Myron's wife Carole, and son Bobby in 1964. The hairstyle of the day was the bee hive.

the life that I lived and, bless her soul, she put up with it. It takes a strong person to be a part of a performer's hectic life. Carole has always handled it like a trouper.

The band started out the New Year with a February 1964, ten-day tour of Canada, again arranged by promoter George Nellis. We meandered through Saskatchewan and Manitoba with entertainer Johnny Tillison ("Poetry In Motion") and The Coasters, along with the Ronnetts ("Be My Baby"). Canadian rock and roll fans remembered The Caddies from when we had toured with Buddy Knox in 1961, which made us feel good. And I was flattered that my record "I Need Someone" was still being played on Canadian radio stations.

In February 1965, I received a welcome call from Bobby Vee. Dick Clark was planning another Caravan of Stars tour starting on he east coast April 30th. Bobby told me that Clark wanted Myron Lee and the Caddies to be part of it again. I was honored, and I accepted the invitation on the spot. Bobby was to be the caravan's headliner again, along with Freddy Cannon, Herman's Hermits, an English group, the Hondells, beautiful Brenda Holloway ("Every Little Bit Hurts"), Little Anthony and The Imperials ("I Think I'm Goin' Out Of My Head"), portly George Lloyd, otherwise known as "Round" Robin, Reparata and the Delrons ("Whenever A Teenager Cries"), the Ikettes, a group with the unusual and squeaky-clean name, The Detergents, George McCannon III, and Billy Stewart.

This time, to my surprise, my photograph was on the advance program that Clark had printed up for the tour. We began to prepare for the tour, rehearsing every day. Because I didn't want to disturb little Bobby at home, we ran through the assigned repertoire at the Arkota Ballroom that Mag Hansen was kind enough to let us use for rehearsing during the week. It wasn't long before we had most of the songs we were to play on the tour down pat.

But the material for Little Anthony and the Imperials was more challenging. Some of their hits had more than the three or four chords that you would usually find in most rock and roll songs. To help us out, the group's musical director spent nearly three hours working with us when we ran through the rehearsals in New York City. He had the music and the chord charts for us, but only the horn players could read the music. The rest of us read the charts and memorized everything as we went along. We had heard their hits many times on the radio, so we had a good idea of the sound.

The two horn men on this second Clark tour were Bob Keys from Texas on the sax and Jim Axelson from Ellendale, MN, who played trumpet and trombone. Bob Keys was an excellent musician and we were glad to have him aboard. Later in the 1960s, after our tour, Bob moved on to the West Coast and joined up with Jimmy Hendricks until Hendricks died of a drug overdose. He then joined The Rolling Stones and for the past twenty-five years he's been with them on tours all over the world.

Our trip to New York this time was in a new, red with red interior 1965 Pontiac station wagon. This '65 Clark tour was similar in many ways to the previous one. Except this time Clark had given me permission to travel in my car and to carry our equipment in our white trailer with "Myron Lee and the Caddies" printed on its sides. On the tour, the two caravan buses always left early for the next engagement to allow time for any emergencies along the way. I reasoned that it would be easier to travel in my car, get some more rest, and leave later. Most of the time it certainly was. There would be an occasion, however, when that wasn't the case.

After the customary rehearsal in New York City, we played some large eastern Canadian cities like Toronto and Montreal. With those shows completed, we followed the buses south, hitting most of the eastern states. It was May 1965, but in the southern states, summer weather was the norm.

Bobby Vee often traded his bus seat with one of my band members and he rode shotgun in my car with us. We enjoyed each other's company and it was great fun cruising to the next date with Bobby along. Once, on a trip of about 250 miles to Ft. Wayne, IN, we dilly-dallied around and left about two hours after the buses took off. We still had plenty of time to get to Ft. Wayne. Unfortunately, we came upon some serious road construction work and detours changed our time schedule.

We drove as fast as we could, but it soon became obvious that we would be a little late. I stopped along the way and called the Ft. Wayne Arena. Luckily, I reached Sarge on the telephone. I apologized and explained our dilemma. He said that to help speed things up, he'd arrange for an Indiana State Trooper to meet us on the west side of Ft. Wayne. As we neared the city, right on time, an Indiana patrol car appeared. "Follow me," the patrolman said. We had a police escort, complete with sirens and flashing lights, all the way to the arena. Even with this help, we were still forty-five minutes late. Dick Clark opened the show in our absence and stalled with his interesting comments for about forty-five minutes until we arrived. With help from others on the tour who were waiting at the stage door, we quickly had our instruments and equipment unloaded and set up on stage during a break after Clark's comments.

The curtain trundled to the stage wings and there was a tremendous roar and loud applause from those who had waited so long. The show went off without a hitch, but I figured that after it ended, there would be hell to pay. But Clark never said a word about it, although I got the distinct impression from the looks I got from Sarge that all did not set well with management. His steely, staring eyes seemed to be saying: "Don't let it happen again, Myron." And it didn't. From then on, we always allowed a little extra time as we traversed from one gig to the next.

Our trip through some of the southern states on that tour was an eye opener for us. As South Dakotans, we had little exposure to the prejudice that manifested itself in many places in the south. It was never evident in the treatment by the fans at our shows when black artists performed. But off the stage in some places in the south in the 1960s, there were cruel examples. In Mississippi, to my surprise, the black artists in the show often had to eat and to stay in places apart from where the rest of us were staying. I was uncomfortable with that arrangement. We worked and traveled with some very kind and talented black artists who also became our close friends. We had never even thought of the racial differences. We were all just musicians trying our best to be good entertainers. Racial harmony has improved greatly since those days, although there is still a long way to go.

Our show on this caravan was arranged so that Freddie "Boom Boom" Cannon, of "Tallahassee Lassie" fame, closed out the first half. Freddie left the fans standing and wanting more. Bobby Vee, as usual, closed the show to thunderous applause. Incidentally, Dell Shannon joined us along the way and performed at some of our stops.

I remember that the Rolling Stones joined us in Philadelphia. By now, a year after we'd first met them at the Texas Teen Fair, the Stones and their music were the rage of the nation. The two buses on the tour and my car were parked inside the large auditorium in Philadelphia, but so many people gathered after the show in hopes of seeing one of the stars that our way out was blocked and we sat for a long time waiting for the crowd to thin out and allow us to drive away.

The tour was over in June and we headed back to good old Sioux Falls and my new family. About this time, the groups from England were crossing the Atlantic in great numbers. Their style of music was gaining in popularity. The American rock and roll scene was never quite the same after that. The Beatles and the Rolling Stones were the new rage. Dick Clark's Caravan of Stars never returned to its early 1960s prominence, although it remained a big draw in subsequent years.

But for those of us who had been privileged to be a part of this historic American music extravaganza during the hay-day of rock and roll, it remains a musical highlight of my life. I will be forever grateful to Bobby Vee for helping make it so, and for Dick Clark's acceptance of our little band of musicians from South Dakota.

10

Rocky Road for Rock and Roll

American rock and roll music took a hit after the Feb. 9, 1964, appearance of The Beatles on the Ed Sullivan television show. The Beatles opened with "All My Lovin'" as the first of five songs during the Sullivan show that was said to have an audience of seventy-three million people. Short hair for men suddenly became passé. The shaggy look was in. American rock and roll wasn't out, but it was down for the count.

By 1966, American rock and roll singers were finding performance dates more difficult to come by. The wonderful ten-year run was ending. The Caddies were not immune from the effects of this tidal wave rolling in on America's shores from England. Opportunities for us and for other rock and roll groups would never again be the same.

My five-year contract with Jimmy Thomas had by now expired. It would not be renewed. I can remember very clearly the details of our discussion on the day Jimmy told me that he could no longer line up dates for the band. We just were not in demand, he said. He could no longer line up a week's worth of work for us by placing a few phone calls, or just waiting for the calls to come in to him. I could also tell by our conversation that Jimmy wasn't happy about the band being on tour so much. There was no commission coming to him when we were gone. He had also begun to book other bands and brought many big name bands to the area, and I couldn't blame him for that. Booking bands was his business.

So with the contract with Jimmy concluded, I decided to take on the booking responsibilities myself. I was young and confident in what the band could do, and I was stubborn. As importantly, I now had a family and I needed to pay the bills. I looked forward to getting into the promotion of shows in this area, fea-

Singer Lou Cristy and Myron Lee between jobs in Denver in 1964. Cristy had several hits, including "Lightening Strikes" and "Keys of Light."

Shorty's Club was a popular night spot in Sioux Falls. It later moved from Eighth Street to a Philips Avenue location where the Cabana Club was once located.

turing big name performers who at times also appeared with the Caddies.

From experience I had learned something about how the business works on both sides of the stage. I began calling around for jobs wherever I could. It's difficult to explain, but imagine that one day you're working with the top names in the music business, performing to screaming fans in huge venues throughout the nation. And then, suddenly, you're calling around to arrange jobs in local clubs and ballrooms, and you're willing to do it for considerably less money than you are used to.

About this time, with music work difficult to find, my drummer Stu Perry left for California for studio work. I couldn't blame him. I could no longer pay salaries and had to pay by the job. Some of those jobs brought in as little as $80, which is what we earned when we played at Shorty's Club in Sioux Falls. Johnnie White had left town and the old Cabana Club was now Shorty's Club. Whatever the name, divide five band members into $80 and that's an indication of the state of things as rock and roll music lost its wind in the late 1960s doldrums.

My very good friend and sax man, Fred Scott, with whom I had shared so much out on the road, couldn't even bring himself to tell me face-to-face that he had to move on. I found his note to me one morning. He thanked me for everything, but said it was time for him to move on. It brought tears to my eyes. I felt that I had let him down. To his credit, bass man Jerry Haacke hung in there with me the longest. But with Fred gone, we were now down to four men, including me. At first, the depleted band sounded empty. It was the first time since I had started out that we were without a sax man. After a while, I became used to the sax-less sound, and my expenses were also less.

Then Jerry Kroon of Madison, SD, our drummer, who had been with us for two years, left us and moved on to Nashville, TN, to pursue his dream. He became a great studio drummer and played on many number one country hits. Over the years, Jerry is still well known as one of the best drummers to ever hit the studios in Nashville. I was in my mid-twenties, but seemingly at the bottom of my venture into the world of music. I've never been a big drinker, but at times it was tempting to seek solace from the bottle. The first time I had even purchased a bottle of whiskey was in Tulsa, OK. We were playing at a fancy club there. It had the elevated stage behind the bar that was the latest rage. People who came didn't dance, but sat at the bar and watched us perform. We were a dance band, not a show band, so I didn't particularly care for the place. But the job was paying good money.

It was during that Oklahoma gig that I started experimenting with booze during our breaks. There was never any drinking before a job. But there was during the breaks. It was just a sip or two. It seemed to settle me down. This innocent flirtation with whiskey was the beginning of what became a very bad habit for a while. Don't get me wrong. I didn't become a falling down, slurred-word drunk or anything even approaching that. I was mindful of what too much liquor could do to a musician. I remembered George Jones and his lonely daytime vigils in his Texas motel room.

Some musicians I knew found relief in what they called speed pills. Dexadrine was among the most popular of these picker-uppers. Musicians called the pills "crossbones" because of the markings on the little white pill that sold on the street for a dime each. The pills helped get them in the mood. I tried it, too, but I never felt good about it. And I was uncomfortable sneaking around popping pills. I found that a drink suited me much better. Over the years, I knew musicians who experimented with marijuana to some degree, but nothing serious. And thank God, it was not to my liking.

My experiment with alcohol and my very brief detour into pills ran counter to the promise I made to myself when I started out. It has always been my philosophy and approach to give what you do your very best shot. When people pay money to see you perform, you need to be capable of doing the very best that you can. Anything less and not only will you not feel good about it, but the audience will soon stop coming.

I must say that I always had fun and tried to enjoy what I was doing. I reminded myself over and over again when I was up on stage not to take myself too seriously. I learned that when I was having fun at work, the people out on the dance floor were enjoying themselves, too. Of course, performers are not immune to injury and illness. I am proud to say that I never missed more than two or three jobs in all of the years I was on the circuit. It wasn't always easy, but I somehow fought my way through the flu, the colds, the headaches, and the other physical roadblocks nature occasionally throws out in front of all of us.

Myron Lee, right, entertains at the Sioux Falls Coliseum in the early 1960s before he brought on the Everly Brothers for forty-five minutes of songs.

When that happens you can't just pick up the phone, call the dance hall manager or convention planner and tell them you won't be there tonight. If physically possible, my approach was to suck it up and do the job. I did that once in spades when the band was hired to play for the KELO-Land Television Christmas party. On the afternoon of the party, I was helping set up our equipment. Suddenly, I felt a stabbing pain in my back. I figured I'd lifted something wrong and had pulled a muscle. It was so painful it bent me over like an old man. On the way home before the party started, I stopped by to see if there was anything my friend and doctor, Mike Hogue, could do for me.

He checked me over and told me I had a kidney stone. He advised that I go to the hospital immediately. That was out of the question because of the KELO-Land party coming up that evening. I asked if I could finish the job, and then go to the hospital later. "That would be okay," he told me, "if you can stand the pain." I had a few drinks before the party and that helped, but it was still a very uncomfortable night. The next morning I checked in at the hospital and was soon on the operating table.

I had started to dabble into promotion of shows, as I mentioned. I signed the Everly Brothers to appear with us at the Sioux Falls Coliseum. The Everlys were riding high with everyone singing along to "Bye, Bye Love." I always felt that they were one of the groups that sounded exactly on stage as they did on their records.

Myron, center, visits with the Everly Brothers, Don, left, and Phil, right, on July 18, 1962, back stage at the dance and performance promoted by Myron that featured the Caddies and headlined the Everlys, at the Sioux Falls Coliseum in 1962. Ticket price set by Myron was $2.50. Even at that price, he said the evening ended as a financial success. The Everlys' fee then for two forty-five minute shows was $1,500.

THE EVERLY BROTHERS	MYRON LEE AND THE CADDIES
JULY 18	WITH
	THE EVERLY BROTHERS
SIOUX FALLS COLISEUM ANNEX	WEDNESDAY, **JULY 18,** 1962
	SIOUX FALLS COLISEUM ANNEX
N⁰ 0360	8 TO 11:30 P.M.
	N⁰ 0360
	PRICE $2.32 · State Tax .05 · Federal Tax .13 · TOTAL $2.50

They had many top forty hits as well as some that were headed for the top of the charts. The Coliseum rent was $150, which I thought a little steep for those days, but I paid it. The price to bring the Everlys to town was even more of a shock—$1,500.

Jimmy Thomas, who got wind of my effort, told me that at $1,500 for the Everlys, I'd lose money. But I had a hunch that the Everlys would be a popular

The Everly Brothers, in black suits, and their band, entertain at a dance that also featured Myron Lee and the Caddies, at the Sioux Falls Coliseum in 1962. The Caddies' rented equipment trailer is in the back with the speakers on top of it. The security guard seated on the amp near the band is Earl Westendorf.

draw. They were. I asked the Odland Music Store and the Sioux Falls Music Store to sell tickets for me at $2. At the Coliseum door, the price was $2.50. Bob Helgeson helped me cut some tapes and I ran those commercials on KIHO in Sioux Falls and KLOH in Pipestone, MN.

I was pumped when the day of the concert arrived. Right on schedule, Don and Phil Everly's big fancy bus pulled into Sioux Falls. With them were three back-up musicians. The Coliseum was packed to the rafters for the show. My band opened the show and got the crowd going. The Everlys then harmonized and chatted through their usual two forty-five minute sets. They did a wonderful job and the fans told them so with raucous applause. I had the opportunity to visit with them back stage and found Don to be a very friendly, outgoing individual. To my mind, his brother Phil, although courteous and polite, seemed a bit standoffish and distant. Maybe he was just having a bad day. The next day I counted my receipts, deducted my expenses, and still had $2,000 left over as net profit. Then, I thought both Phil and Don were tremendous. Promoting, I figured, was going to be a very profitable part of the music business. I would soon learn otherwise.

Flushed with that concert's success, I brought Ray Stevens and Buddy Knox to Sioux Falls. Because of timing or a break down in promotion or something, I barely broke even. Next came the biggest promotion blunder of my life similar to the "Peter Rabbit" debacle. I decided a show on New Year's Eve would be very popular in Sioux Falls. Bobby Vinton came to town for that one. His song, "Roses are

Myron Lee appeared with The Everly Brothers in a 1962 dance and concert at the Coliseum in Sioux Falls, and teenagers sought him out for his autograph.

Myron brought singer Bobby Vinton to a New Year's Eve show at the Sioux Falls Coliseum in the early 1960s when Vinton's "Roses Are Red" was a number one hit.

```
          MYRON LEE PRESENTS
                 YOUR
         NEW YEARS EVE DANCE PARTY
                STARRING
              BOBBY VINTON
        SIOUX FALLS COLISEUM ANNEX
                9 — 1 P.M.
            MONDAY DEC. 31st 1962
                                    $1.79
                              Federal Tax  .08
   N⁰   0014     Advance      State Tax    .04
                              Auditorium   .09
                 Prices       TOTAL $2.00
```

```
          MYRON LEE PRESENTS
                 YOUR
         HALLOWEEN DANCE PARTY
                  with
              NEIL SEDAKA
        SIOUX FALLS COLISEUM ANNEX
              8 TO 11:30 P.M.
           WEDNESDAY OCT. 31st 1962
                                    $1.79
                              Federal Tax  .08
   N⁰    414     Advance      State Tax    .04
                              Auditorium   .09
                 Prices       TOTAL $2.00
```

Red," was flying high. I invested several hundred dollars to have the Coliseum decorated for a thunderous year-ender. We hung giant nets filled with balloons from the ceiling to be released at midnight and cascade down on the thousands of party-goers that we expected. It would be one successful New Year's shebang, I thought. We again opened that show and Vinton did his agreed-upon two sets with a band called The Bellnotes that he'd brought with him.

The night was pretty much of a bust. I had misjudged everything. Alcohol wasn't allowed in the Coliseum. Most people going out on New Year's Eve have consumption as a primary mission. Everyone except Myron Lee was probably aware of that.

Only about five hundred people showed up. What they paid for tickets was not enough to meet my expenses. But I learned a good lesson. Never plan a New Year's Eve show where amenities are not allowed. After paying Vinton his $1,000 and sending off checks for rent, balloons, the printing of tickets and my other expenses, I began to realize that promoting shows was more challenging and a bigger risk than I had first assumed. It was turning out to be a quick way to lose money.

But as a stubborn German, I am apparently also a slow learner. I tried my promoting luck again, bringing in Neil Sedaka, who was enjoying numerous hits on the charts. Again, the take from that concert was just enough to break even.

During that same period, I had bookings for my band in the Black Hills, playing in Spearfish about every six weeks. I asked Jerry Sternad, the Spearfish Pavilion operator, if he would be interested in joining with me in bringing the Everly Brothers to town. We'd be equal partners. He was reluctant to join with me in the venture after he learned that the Everlys were a $1,500 package. But he did offer to rent the Pavilion to me for just $150.

I paid the rent and brought the Everlys to Spearfish in the summer of 1963. To help keep travel costs for my band down, I booked us in Gregory, SD, on the Friday night before the Everlys' Saturday night show. After the Gregory dance ended in the wee hours of Saturday, we headed for Spearfish. That evening when we got to the Pavilion, people were already lining up to buy tickets.

Curt Powell, who was the Caddies very first guitar player, was tuning up and was playing a few licks before the show when Don Everly walked in and looked me up. Don asked me where I had found "that guy," nodding toward Curt. I told him Curt was an old friend from Sioux Falls. Don shook his head in disbelief and said he'd never heard anyone that good, except for Chet Atkins, with whom the Everlys had recorded in Nashville on several occasions. I wasn't surprised that Curt had impressed the Everlys. He got that reaction everywhere we went. It was nice to have such a great talent in the band. He died in the summer of 2003, but in my mind, he was the best technical guitar player I have ever heard anywhere, and he was certainly as good as any of the nation's best on that instrument.

At about 7 p.m. my brother-in-law Larry Westendorf, who came along to help me sell tickets, opened the little ticket booth similar to something you'd find at a theater. People were shoving their money in to us as fast as we could take it and hand them back change and a ticket. We soon had the booth's two money drawers stuffed with bills, and the line of anxious fans was still pressing in on us. To keep the line moving along, we started throwing the ones and five dollar bills on the floor. We were locked in the place so security wasn't a problem. The fluttering greenbacks began building up on the floor like drifting snow. Soon we were wallowing ankle deep in money. It was a great feeling. From the corner of my eye as I made change, I could see Jerry Sternard standing nearby, salivating and probably wishing that he'd partnered with me. If he had, several inches of those bills on the floor would have been his.

The Everlys, as usual, turned in an excellent show on that hot night in Spearfish. The people in the crowd seemed to know every word of every song and mouthed the words and swayed to the music.

After the show and the dance, we packed up and drove back to Sioux Falls in the early-morning hours of Sunday. In the trunk were a couple of suitcases stuffed with money. It was one of the most pleasant rides across a darkened South Dakota that I've ever had.

That fall I promoted two more dances in Spearfish. The first was Jerry Lee Lewis, who recorded "Whole Lotta Shakin' Goin' On," "Great Balls of Fire," and many other big hits. The Killer, as he had been called since childhood because of his wild lifestyle, charged $850, or fifty percent of the gate, whatever was greater. I'd seen him perform many times on television and a few times live. He was always very good. He wasn't exactly Mr. Personality off stage, in my opinion, but I didn't know him well. He traveled with what I perceived to be a rather strange cadre of camp followers, but he did attract big crowds and also put on a good show. He's nearly seventy years old now, but still has a wide following and a loyal, enthusiastic fan club.

In mid-winter of 1965 I hired Conway Twitty to do a show in Spearfish. He had not yet immersed himself into the county music business, but he had a string of rock and roll hits under this belt. I particularly admired his song "It's Only Make Believe." Interestingly, Conway had the same booking agent as Jerry Lee Lewis and his price was also $850 or fifty percent of the take. I thought Conway was much more polished than Lewis and deserved to be in a little higher pay grade. He was very business-like and surrounded himself with great musicians. I was surprised when Conway told me that he had driven his station wagon pulling a rented U-Haul all the way from Arkansas to

Myron promoted a Conway Twitty appearance at a dance in Spearfish, and this is the photo Twitty sent to him for advertising purposes.

Spearfish. I remember thinking that he must have really needed the work to come all that way into the teeth of a Dakota winter, for the price he was to be paid. Not long after his Spearfish show, he switched his image to country music and went on to record over fifty number one hits. It wasn't long before he had a big jet instead of a U-Haul trailer, and underlings to handle his luggage and equipment. Perhaps that change in his music style was also due to the emerging popularity of the music being done The Beatles way.

For the Twitty show, I hired my Larchwood, IA, flying instructor Russ Zangger to fly some of us across the state to Spearfish. Russ had a Tri-Pacer big enough to carry myself, my brother-in-law Larry, who would again help sell tickets, and Chico Hajek, our drummer. The other guys drove out. We left from the Sioux Falls Airport and the flight was uneventful and enjoyable, with a bright sun and a beautiful, snow-dappled South Dakota landscape below. The temperature was near zero.

After we landed at the Spearfish Airport, Russ arranged to have the plane parked inside a hangar away from the wind and the snow. The airport crew and Russ set a barrel cut in half under the Tri-Pacer's engine. Some briquettes in it were glowing and the heat would keep the airplane's engine warm enough for a quick start later that night when we were ready to leave. Russ elected to spend his time at a nearby motel. I doubt if he even knew Conway Twitty was performing. And even if he did, I don't think he had any idea who Conway Twitty was. He was more interested in flying, and getting some rest before the flight back to Sioux Falls after our show.

Conway drew a great West River crowd that night and I paid him $1,100, which was his fifty percent share. As I was paying him off he mentioned that he and his crew were staying overnight in Spearfish. I told him that some of us would be flying back to Sioux Falls as soon as everything was packed and ready. Conway and I stood outside as a dusting of snow fell. The temperature hovered around the twenty-below mark. It was Greenland cold! We shook hands and bid one another farewell. He turned as if to leave, then stopped and came back. In a very serious voice he told me that he didn't think it would be a good idea to be flying that night. He said he'd lost friends who braved the elements when they shouldn't have, referring to the Buddy Holly disaster. I assured him that our pilot was excellent and that he had an instrument rating.

We left the Pavilion with ballroom operator Jerry Sternard driving, and picked up Russ at the motel. He was dressed for the winter, heavy cap with ear floppers, thermo-underwear, heavy gloves, and the whole nine yards. Unfortunately, his passengers were dressed for comfort under stage lights in a dancehall. We had no hats, no gloves, and wore light clothing. Not anticipating what was in store for us, Larry cadged a couple of pillows and a blanket from Russ' motel room. We got to the Spearfish Airport three miles from town at about 2:30 a.m. By now the wind had picked up and was stirring the light snow. I knew it was cold because when we walked the snow crunched, a sure sign in South Dakota.

Just as we were preparing to board, Conway and his guitar player, Big Joe, drove up. They walked over to us. Conway once again told me he had a bad feeling about us flying that night. "Myron," Conway, said, shaking his head, "I've had friends killed in these damm little planes and I don't think tonight is a good flying night. I beg you, please wait until tomorrow." I was touched by his sincere concern for our safety and for taking the time to drive out to warn me. But I wasn't in the least concerned about the flight. I had every confidence in Russ' flying knowledge and ability. He'd been my flight instructor several years earlier. In fact, on my solo flight at his school in Larchwood, IA, I'd messed up one of his airplanes.

I could have been killed in that one, but injuries to my body were minor. It was my ego that suffered the most. Back then, coming in for my solo landing, a fence line near the end of the runway seemed to reach up and grab the airplane's tail wheel and the plane pancaked unceremoniously smack dab onto a railroad track near the end of the runway. The plane was destroyed and I was shaken, but alive. To add insult to injury, a freight train heading for Sioux Falls was approaching at the time and was forced to stop until I and the remains of the slick little airplane were removed from the tracks. Since I wasn't at the controls as we left Spearfish that cold night, I knew we all were in very good hands and I had no concerns.

As we taxied to the runway, I glanced out the frosted window and saw Twitty and Big Joe in their car, watching us leave. We had an interesting take off, bouncing over and through small finger-drifts packed hard by the wind. But we were finally airborne and lifted off into a steep climb. The windows now were completely fogged over and Russ was on instruments. I was still rather nonchalant about the flight. Russ, probably amused, looked over and asked me if I could recall "if that peak we saw when we came in was on the right or on the left."

The little 120 horsepowered engine was working hard for us, but it didn't send much heat our way because of the extreme outside temperature, especially at altitude. It was uncomfortably cold in the cockpit. Chico and Larry in the backseat were wrapped up like cocoons in the blanket we'd "appropriated" from the motel. We climbed to 8,000 feet. Up there, the air was crystal clear, and also crystal cold. Russ teased a flashlight beam across the instrument panel and then out his window, now clear of fog. It illuminated a thermometer on a wing strut. It was forty degrees below zero out there, and probably only a little warmer in the cockpit. It was so cold that Russ took pity on us and decided to land in Pierre to allow all of us time to thaw out. Then we were off again, headed for the glow on the horizon that was Sioux Falls off to the southeast.

Because of the strong tail winds, the 400-mile flight back to Sioux Falls only took about two and one-half hours, but it was the most miserable 150 minutes of our lives. After landing in Sioux Falls, Russ taxied over near to where my car was parked. I hoisted myself out of the airplane as best I could. I hit the ground and discovered I couldn't walk on my nearly frozen feet. I literally crawled on my hands and knees to my car. Fortunately, the motor kicked over and started. We just sat there shivering until the heater began to share some warmth and we watched as Russ took off for his home base in Larchwood, IA, near my infamous crash site.

A few years later I asked Russ if he remembered that polar trip. "Were you ever worried?" I asked. He admitted that there were times when he wondered if we should have taken Twitty's advice. (Incidentally, Twitty, a wonderful man and tremendous entertainer, died on June 5, 1993, on his sixtieth birthday, in Branson, MO.) Given the hundreds of thousands of miles I've traveled by car, airplane, and even by boat, I have always felt blessed that I have not been involved in any serious accidents.

My last foray into the promotional world was in 1964 when I booked the popular television show called "The Hootenanny." It was made popular by Jack Linkletter, son of Art Linkletter. A "hootenanny," I was to learn, was another name for a show of songs. Groups like The Lettermen and the Kingston Trio and others created something of a folk music revival, and the word "hootenanny" came with all of that. The Hootenanny show started touring the country and featured a group called The Big Three, that included Tim Rose, John Brown, and a young lady named Cass Elliot, who later became popularly known as Mama Cass.

I thought The Hootenanny would be a gold mine in Sioux Falls. I dug deep and paid $500 to rent the Sioux Falls Arena. I invested more in extensive advertising. But even that didn't save the show. The Hootenanny turned out to be a real flapjack flop in Sioux Falls. I decided to bow out gracefully from my career in promoting and go back to doing what I did best.

The music scene was changing. Work wasn't that easy to find. I had to change some of my ways.

11

Stepping Back and Moving Forward

By far the most trying, difficult time for me was during the period 1966 to 1975. Carole and I welcomed our second child, Kelli, on June 7, 1966, but this joyous moment also came with the realization that my music work was falling off.

Carole decided—and correctly so—to quit her part-time job at the telephone company so that she could be home to devote more time to raising the children. Paying our bills became increasingly difficult from the money I was making with my music. I began thinking about getting a regular job. It was something I'd never had since my boyhood days delivering papers, and I never thought of my music as a job.

I'd been out on the road for seven years, enjoying the time and earning good money from engagements of every sort in venues of every kind from coast to cost and all the other stops in between. So a regular job with regular hours would be a new experience for me. It would also be a psychological hurdle I knew I had to clear. I was secretly embarrassed and I hoped no one would know that I had to work for a living. I think people who knew me thought I had bundles of money from my work in music buried in a cream can out in my backyard somewhere. So it was a difficult time for me. My ego was bruised; I felt ashamed that I perhaps had failed in the music business. It took me several months to sort out those concerns before I realized that social factors over which I had no control had brought about the changes in the music of the day.

Fortunately I found work at KELO television as a studio cameraman. I was making about $5 an hour, which was more than the minimum wage, but didn't begin to match the paychecks I had become used to getting. But the work and the pay were steady and were keeping the wolf from our door. The KELO job had

99

other advantages, too. I started each morning at 5:30 a.m. and was off by 2 p.m. so I could help at home and also spend afternoons on the telephone trying to line up music jobs. The studio job was away from the public in a controlled situation, so most of the people who knew me would not be aware that I was working and in somewhat dire financial straights. The folks at KELO were helpful and wonderful workmates and I valued their friendship.

I also discovered that I enjoyed the work and having the weekends off so that I could play the few music dates I was able to arrange. KELO soon promoted me to audio engineer. I sat alone in a sound booth. A friend from high school, Al Oveson, was the video engineer. We were both there to sign on the station each weekday at 5:30 a.m. I remained at KELO for two years, during which Al and I struck up a lasting friendship.

I then received an offer in 1968 to work for Stich's Cycle and Marine for slightly more than what I was making at KELO. At Stich's I sold everything from bikes to boats and snowmobiles. My childhood friend, Chuck Molter, whose dad had given The Caddies our first out-of-town job at Tyndall, worked at Stich's, and I grew up knowing all of the members of the Stich family. I'd gotten used to having a real job and I enjoyed working there. It was a part of my life for thirteen years. During the first winter at Stich's, in 1968, incidentally, Sioux Falls was buried in over one hundred inches of snow, so I had a rewarding baptism in the fine art of selling snowmobiles. Still, getting into the groove at Stich's wasn't easy. There was always music being piped into Stich's building, and often when I heard a singer with whom I had worked, I wondered what in the heck I was doing there selling snowmobiles.

During this time, our third child, son Kris Myron, was born Dec. 4, 1972. My wife and I are big Minnesota Viking football fans, and the day Kris decided to join us was also the day the Vikings were playing. Early in the game Carole began to experience labor pains and finally called Dr. Milton Mutch. He advised her to come to the hospital. She asked if she couldn't remain at home until the Viking game was over. His answer was a stern no. He finally agreed that she could bring a portable black and white television set to the hospital with her and she could watch it in the delivery room if necessary. He said he'd never done that before. So I took Carole to the hospital and, at Carole's urging since the pains had subsided, I then returned home to rejoin our guests, Roger and Arlene Reynolds, and settled in to watch the rest of the Viking game. After the game, I went back to the hospital, and when it came time for Carole to go into the delivery room, I asked Dr. Mutch if I might go in, too, and observe the birth of our child. He handed me a mask and a gown and told me to stand back out of the way. It was a wonderful experience for me to watch Kris being born.

Meanwhile, back at Stich's during the 1970s, my son Bob and I became interested in ham radio. Jim Meert, a good friend, taught us the basics, and we eventually received our General Class licenses and could then transmit and receive both coded and voice radio signals. I set up a cozy little radio shack in my basement, invested in some of the basic bells and whistles including a fifty-foot tower outside our country home, and spent long hours talking to people all over the world.

The experience improved my speaking abilities while staring at a microphone, so it helped me in my music business, too. And it was one of the reasons I decided to apply for a job at KKFN Radio in Sioux Falls in the late 1980s. Having a radio program was something I had always thought would be enjoyable to do since my growing up years when I listened to the popular Sioux Falls announcer Wayne Pritchard.

Mornings before school at our house, Mom always had the dial set for KSOO and Wayne Pritchard. So all through the 1950s and 1960s, I listened to his very able and familiar voice, and came to admire what he did and how he did it. Much later in life, I met him in person at the YMCA where we were both relaxing in the steam room. With free time during the day because of evening engagements, I developed the habit of spending time at the YMCA every day. (By the way, joining the Sioux Falls YMCA at a young age was one of the best decisions I have ever made.) When I met Wayne, I told him of my admiration for what he did, and that he'd been a familiar voice in our home all during my growing up years. We became pretty good friends after that and talked about music and the band and many other things. He wasn't a big rock and roll fan and once said that the music was "terrible." He told me that the good music died with the end of the big band days. I told him that I wish that he felt otherwise about my kind of music, but that I could certainly understand his loyalty to the music of his youth, too. I was saddened, as were so many thousands of fans in Sioux Falls and the surrounding area, when we lost Wayne in 2003. He was certainly an important personality in the long history of Sioux Falls radio.

With my radio confidence built up by the ham radio experience, and with the ownership of Stich's Cycle and Marine having changed hands, I applied for a job at KKFN Radio in 1989. The general manager, Linda Johnson, was very kind and understanding during our interview, but she told me that there were no openings at that time. She was familiar with Myron Lee and the Caddies, however, and suggested that with my musical background, I should put together a ten-minute musical trivia show that could be pre-recorded and aired five days a week. The hooker was that I'd have to find my own sponsor. The idea sounded interesting, so I began looking for a sponsor. I was fortunate to know the people who owned the local Coca-Cola dealership, Jim and Tom Nelsen, and they generously agreed to underwrite the show. It became one of the most enjoyable projects of my life.

I started writing the shows and convinced Roger Reynolds, who so ably handled the sound for my band, to help me. He had a small recording studio in his basement where we would record a week's worth of programs on Monday afternoons.

On each program, I picked out some famous rock and roll artist as the featured subject. I included biographical data on the artist and played one or two of the artist's hit songs, then closed the segment by asking a question about some trivial information mentioned during the ten-minute show. When the segment played on air later, the on-air personality would take calls from listeners. Interestingly, the prize to the winner was $12.30, which was a take on the station's spot on the dial, 1230 AM. To my surprise, the little show, called Myron Lee's Trivia, was an immediate success.

Myron Lee and the Caddies' Gary Swanson, left, Rick Burkhardt, center, and Dwight Green, right, posing with Myron for a picture taken at the Sioux Falls Elks Club in the late 1970s.

About six months after it was launched, Linda offered me a chance to be live on the station's 6 a.m. to 10 a.m. show that was formatted for commuters and those in kitchens preparing for their day. It was a combination talk show and 1950s and 1960s music show. My partner was Jerry Richards. I accepted without a second thought, and although I am sure now that I was probably not all that good at first, I had a ball. Of course, Jerry's expertise carried us through.

Myron's radio talk show co-host Ugly Dell (Dell Mullroy) with The Caddies' sound man Roger Reynolds at Husset's Speedway in Sioux Falls in 1991.

After a few weeks with Jerry, Linda informed me that she had hired a radio personality from the Minneapolis market to team up with me on the show. His name was Dell Mullroy, whose radio name was Ugly Dell. Curious about my proposed new partner, I called Bobby Vee, who lived north of Minneapolis. Bobby said he was somewhat familiar with Ugly Dell and gave him a thumb's up.

Dell was an impressive character. Not only did he stand six feet, six inches tall and weigh in at three hundred pounds, he possessed very unconventional work habits. During the five days each week he worked at the station before he rested on the weekends, he lived in his car. I've often tried to picture a man of that mass existing in a little four-door car. I'm still not at all sure just how he did it. But he did. From time to time, he might spend a night at one of those inexpensive hotels that were out East Tenth Street. But mostly he was at home in his car, from which he would alight each weekday morning at about 5:55 a.m. disheveled, bedraggled, and hungry, to begin our 6 a.m. program.

Ugly Dell apparently hadn't worked with a partner before, so our inaugural program was rather stilted and sluggish. He must have known of my lack of experience in the radio business, too. One of my studio responsibilities was to handle the telephone, and many of the calls over the next several weeks were not complimentary of Ugly Dell. He was good, but the big city market had influenced his on-air personality. He needed to adjust his style out here on the flatlands. He talked too fast and he seemed to relate his comments and interests more to the Twin Cities than to Sioux Falls. I didn't mention the negative phone calls to him, but I soon concluded that it was just too difficult to work with the man. We didn't seem to connect. I told the station manager I wanted out. Linda encouraged me to give the partnership more time. Only later did I learn that Ugly Dell had made a similar visit to Linda's office, and felt about me as I felt about him.

I gradually came to the conclusion that I needed to be honest with Ugly Dell. I told him what the listeners where calling about. Knowing that a 300-pounder might suddenly land heavily on my chest, I took a deep breath and suggested he might try to improve his on-air persona with our Sioux Falls listeners. Surprisingly, he took my advice very well, and even seemed to appreciate my honesty. Within days we were working as a team. We were having more fun on the air. The Ugly Dell and Myron Show was attracting more and more listeners. Soon, Chuck Staudenmaier, the general manager of the big Sioux Falls Vern Eide auto dealership, recognized our drawing power and purchased an advertising package for the entire year.

We did live remotes from the Vern Eide car lots and people who drove by in the morning rush hour would stop to talk or honk as they passed by on the streets. Soon, another big sponsor, Dashboard Electronics, joined us. It was amazing what a one hundred-sixty pound guitar player and a three hundred pound car live-in accomplished. After our first year, in 1990, the station's ratings went from the bottom of the pit to near the top of the morning market. The Vern Eide dealership even made a new car available for our use. Fortunately, it was a Honda. Ugly Dell didn't fit in it that well, which didn't disappoint me in the least. I had the new car all to myself.

Our show format was unscripted and amounted to just breezy conversations between Ugly Dell and me, talking about our childhoods and the good old days. He was 45 years old and I was 48, so we could relate very well. Of course, with Ugly Dell, the subject often revolved around food, too. We accidentally discovered that our food dissertations had an unintended, but welcome consequence. If we talked about hamburgers, some business would send over a dozen to the studio for us to enjoy. Once we talked about lobster, and the Red Lobster franchise sent us a lobster dinner for two.

We'd try anything on the air so long as it was in good taste. Once, I did a live remote from a hot air balloon drifting over the city. Ugly Dell had been invited along, but he wasn't sure about the laws of physics that pitted a three hundred pound man against the forces of hot air, and stayed on the ground. I was secretly relieved, since I didn't know what an extra three hundred pounds would do to a balloon wicker basket, either.

Soon, folks were coming down to the radio studio to watch us at work. Often, we'd call one of the famous rock and roll artists that either Ugly Dell or I knew, and have on-air interviews. The joy of the show was that neither of us knew what we would be doing during the program that day. We just winged it, and we were very successful with that approach. Everyone was listening. I remember that the folks at Vern Eide told me that they checked the radio dials of the used cars they took in as trades. A high percentage of drivers were turned to the 1230 AM frequency.

In 1990, the station brought a rock and roll show to town. One of the stars was Fabian. He was to appear at the Howard Johnson Convention Center. I was given the assignment of picking Fabian up at the airport when his private jet arrived from

California the night before the event. I decided to take with me two avid rock and roll fans and good friends, Harold and Carol Geist. They had attended our dances since we first started out. They are wonderful people and fabulous dancers. The Geists also had a snazzy, refurbished 1960 Impala, a red convertible that I thought would fit into the theme of the rock and roll event. I asked the Geists if they would mind providing transportation for Fabian. At the airport, Harold was the perfect chauffer and his wife Carol rode in the back seat with Fabian, who got a big kick out of his ride back in time to the Holiday Inn, where he stayed that night.

In 1991, new ownership took over at KKFN and changed the format from music to news. Ugly Dell returned to the Twin Cities area and I was jobless again except for my music business, which thank God was very good again and improving every week. I loved the radio job and hated to lose it, but my band was hot again during the 1980s and the money began rolling in again. In fact, 1989 was one of the best years I ever had. The old 1960s music had been making a comeback and people associated my band with that genre.

Before Ugly Dell left, he told me he'd never had such a good time in radio. I told him I hadn't either. After we parted and went our separate ways, we kept in touch and were the closest of friends. In 2002, Ugly Dell, who by now had abandoned his car-living habits, returned to his home after his Saturday night radio show in Minneapolis, retired for the night and never woke up again. To me, he will always be my friend Dell Mullroy, not Ugly Dell.

Through the years, even when I held regular jobs in Sioux Falls, I continued to get a smattering of music dates at places within a couple hundred miles of Sioux Falls. While at Stich's in 1969, I received a call from Lucille, who ran the Sir Richard's Club out on West Twelfth Street near Skunk Creek. She offered $250 for the band to play on weekends from September through May. I was thrilled to accept. One of the nice things about the Sir Richard's job was that we could leave our equipment there on stage, all set up and ready to go. This was a blessing for us and for my aching back after years of setting up and tearing down, then driving hither and thither to the next date.

The band was now a four-piece group. To save money, I opted to not have a horn man. With me were Gordon Underwood, bass, Ron Neuberger, lead guitar, and Chuck Spawn, drums. Word spread that the Caddies were back, and the crowds at Sir Richards grew with each passing weekend. On most Saturday nights, people were lined up waiting to get in. Lucille was happy with the added business, and in her glory sitting at the front door collecting the $1 cover charge. In those days, Sir Richard's sold set-ups for fifty cents. Everyone brought their own liquor and paid for glasses of ice and the mix of their choice. The place had a nice steak house attached to the lounge, so it was a regular one-stop entertainment center.

When we started playing there it was difficult for me to get back in the groove. I'd become spoiled by our first go-round in the music business in the late 1950s and early 1960s. Then it was my life and it was a part of me twenty-four hours a day. Now, with the responsibility of a family and a regular day job, music occupied an important niche, but it wasn't my total being. Each weekend, however, I was able to open the old guitar case and music and entertaining again became fun and important to me. I gradually adjusted to this new chapter in my life. It wasn't long before I looked forward to the weekends and seeing the host of friends I was making at Sir Richard's. Many in the crowd became regulars and it was like old home week every weekend. It became a tradition that after the place closed, the band and dozens of fans and friends headed for Kirk's Restaurant at Twelfth and Kiwanis or Sambo's on East Tenth Street for an early breakfast. It wasn't unusual for me to get home around 3 a.m.

I began to look forward to playing at Sir Richard's. People today still talk about the fun they had there. In my mind's eye, I can still see the faces of the people at Sir Richard's enjoying the dancing and the fun. I see people I've known now for years whom I met there. Many rarely missed a Saturday night at Sir Richard's, including Buddy and Clair, Russ and Marlene Grady, Dick and Sharon Stich and all of the Stich crew, Dean and Jan Everetts, and Les and Coletta Bly, to name just a few.

Sir Richard's is where I met Roger and Arlene Reynolds, and they ended up working with the band for over twenty-five years, handling the sound, doing what they could to help and just being good friends. They were very important to the band as we climbed back to popularity in the 1980s.

Sometimes, since Carole and I lived on Suncrest Road a few blocks from Sir Richard's, we invited friends over after the club closed. If the weather allowed, we grilled steaks and played volleyball until dawn in our backyard illuminated with lights I'd strung up in our trees. Fortunately, the neighbors were understanding of our early morning transgressions, and never complained.

The crowds at Sir Richard's were great and I think just about everyone in Sioux Falls came out to dance and to listen to us. I was starting to get calls for music dates again. The Caddies were so successful in drawing crowds to Sir Richard's that Lucille kept us gainfully employed there for three years. When she died at the

Two of Myron's longtime friends on the road were and still are Arlene and Roger Reynolds. Here Arlene is running the stage lights and Roger the sound equipment. This picture was taken in 1991 at a Hurley, SD, street dance.

beginning of our third year, her daughter took over the club. Even as important as the Sir Richard's job was in bringing me back to my roots, it was also valuable as a stepping-stone on the long, slow climb back up again in the local and regional music scene.

After being more or less out of action for several years, even by 1975 I began to fill my book with playing dates again. We played the Sioux Falls Elks Lodge every six weeks. Erv Pfeifer was the Elks Club manager then, and he built it into a very successful place. We had large crowds at our dances for many, many years. Convention dates began to come in, too. Soon, we were packing crowds at the Moose Lodge every six to eight weeks. It seemed the more people who saw us and heard us, the more calls I received. In fact, business became so good that I never had to call for a job again for over fifteen years. People called me.

In the mid-1970s one of our enjoyable jobs was playing for fund raising dances sponsored by the Catholic Churches in Sioux Falls—specifically, the combined parishes of St. Joseph's, St. Lambert's, St. Mary's, St. Theresa's, and St. Michael's. The crowds were large. Being raised as a Lutheran, I was also surprised that Catholics were good dancers, too, and knew how to have fun. For a few years the dances were held in the O'Gorman High School gymnasium or at the Arkota Ballroom. The St. Michael's dances later moved to the Ramkota Convention Center because it had out-grown the O'Gorman gym, and, some said, the gym began taking on the aroma of a very busy bar for days after the event. We enjoyed working with Fr. James Doyle and the others, and were grateful when they credited the band as the main reason for the large crowds. My Dad had been a Catholic, but, as I mentioned, Mom had raised us kids as Lutherans. One day, I joked with Fr. Doyle that perhaps deep down I was actually a Catholic because my Lutheran brethren sure didn't give me the dance business his church did.

Dances such as those sponsored by the church, and many others, are so enjoyable for musicians and performers. You get such a wonderful feeling, an unexplainable "high," from seeing the joy and happiness and fielding the compliments and the applause. The pay for what you do is incidental, really. The adrenalin flows and for hours and often even days afterwards you have a satisfied feeling for having been responsible for helping so many people have fun and enjoy themselves. Often I'd come home early in the morning after a dance, put on a pot of coffee and just sit alone in the kitchen reliving in my mind the music and the people I'd met, deep in pleasant thoughts and happy memories. Once, returning home at 2 or 3 a.m., I pulled the car over and just sat there for over an hour alone in my thoughts, enjoying the peace and quiet and the stars and thinking about what a wonderful profession I was in.

It isn't always milk and honey, however. Sometimes, that satisfied feeling after a night of playing is absent. Take for example the night of July 7, 1984. We were playing at Barry Bare's Westport Lounge just east of the Target store on Westport Avenue. We were there often in the early 1980s. On this particular night, an older couple that had heard that we would be at the Westport was in the audience. In fact, they had called me earlier to inquire about what kind of place the Westport Lounge was. I assured them that it was not a rough dive at all, but a nice lounge that

This poster was used by Myron Lee and the Caddies in the late 1980s. From left are Gary Swanson, Richard Burkhardt, Dave Severson, with Myron Lee in front.

attracted nice people. I told them they would surely enjoy themselves. I even invited them to be my guests, arranging a table for them near the stage.

After the first set, I joined them at their table, bought them a drink, and we talked. They agreed that the evening was progressing nicely, and that they were having fun. I returned to the stage for the next set. As we played, I periodically glanced down at my special guests to be sure they were being treated like kings. It was still fairly early in the evening. I was singing Roy Orbison's "Pretty Woman" when I heard what sounded like a couple of well-placed rim shots and I thought they were by our drummer, Gary Swanson. The rim shots, however, were out of time and not at an appropriate place in the song. I looked around questionably at Gary. He shrugged his shoulders as if to tell me he had no idea what happened either.

Right away the club manager came on stage and asked us to page for a doctor. After we'd played another tune, we were told to stop by policemen who were fully armed when they entered the lounge. I'd noticed some commotion in a booth a short distance from the stage moments before, but it was difficult to see because of the spotlights aimed at the stage. I hadn't heard anything because of our music, except of course the misplaced "rim shots," so didn't suspect anything too serious. Soon, a cop came up on stage and told me that there had been a shooting. I was to announce to the crowd that no one would be allowed to leave until the officers had questioned everyone.

It was then that I learned that a man in a nearby booth had been shot in the head at close range, and killed. I looked down at the older couple who came to the lounge on my sterling recommendation and assurance. They looked scared to death. All of us in the room waited for about two hours until the questioning was completed.

Later, when I walked out to my car that evening after it was all over, I noticed a large yellow "X" painted on the pavement near my car. A policeman nearby told me that the "X" marked where they had found a spent cartridge. I later learned that the trouble was a dispute between a biker and someone else. The biker, named Paul, had been shot in the head as he sat in the Westport Lounge booth. He died a short time later. A friend of the man who was shot, who had been in the booth with him, followed the shooter outside and fired at him as he ran through the parking lot. The spent cartridge by my car was a result of that rolling gun fight. It had been quite a night at the Westport. Incidentally, I never again received a telephone call from the older couple, and I never noticed them out in the audience of the Westport Lounge again, either.

While on the subject of events in some of the Sioux Falls lounges, I must tell you about the interesting night at the Blackwatch. I wasn't playing there at the time, but was there as a guest of the Lawrence Welk Stars who had presented a show at the Coliseum earlier that evening. It was in the late 1980s.

My friend Dr. Mike Hogue called and gleefully announced that he had tickets and a back stage pass for that Lawrence Welk Stars show. By this time, Lawrence had retired and some of the stars of the show were on tour without the entire Welk contingent. Dr. Mike knew I liked the Welk band and thought of me when his uncle, who worked as some sort of advance man for the stars of the show, gave him the tickets. Of course, I couldn't ignore doctor's orders, so I gladly agreed to go along with him.

It was a wonderful night at the Coliseum. Here we were, my good doctor and I, walking around backstage much in awe, rubbing shoulders with such awesome talent. Among the stars who were there were Ralna, JoAnne Castle, the bouncing blond piano player, the great clarinet player Henry Cuesta, and Joe Feeney, the sweet Irish tenor with the cherubic face. The show was over by about 9:30 p.m. One of Welk's people asked Dr. Mike and I where they might go for a nice quiet nightcap, and a place to unwind. They were all staying at the Townhouse Motel so we agreed that the Blackwatch Lounge next door was the place. We were invited to join them, and we fell all over ourselves accepting.

It was a weeknight and this cut down on the customer numbers at the Blackwatch. We had the place almost to ourselves. But word must have filtered out, because a good crowd of Welk fans gradually filtered in as the evening progressed.

Mike and I were seated at a table with Ralna, who was no longer married to her singing partner, Guy. We enjoyed the conversation and her stories and descriptions of what it was like being a part of a show of such stature.

Across the room was JoAnne Castle. I had met her out on the East Coast while we were touring with Bobby Vee in 1962. We all were doing the grandstand show at the Pennsylvania State Fair and I had an opportunity to visit with her backstage. I ask her what it was like working for such an icon as Welk. She wrinkled her nose, shrugged, and indicated that he was not known for his generosity in paying those who worked for him. She was somewhat uncomplimentary of him in other ways, too, and said she received union scale for her time during rehearsals and a little bit more for the actual taping of the Welk show. I'm sure that if one were to ask her about her former boss today, she'd be more generous, because Lawrence Welk made her career for her. But in 1962 while waiting to go on the Pennsylvania State Fair stage, what did any of us know?

Back at the Blackwatch, Dr. Mike and I were in awe of our visiting dignitaries. The evening was progressing in fine fashion when suddenly all hell broke loose. It seems JoAnne Castle and Joe Feeney were engaged in a noisy disagreement. I never did find out what sparked the animated discussion.

They were loud and the language wasn't something you'd write home about. Although Joe Feeney had the stage persona of the sweet Irish boy next door, he didn't exhibit that image at the Blackwatch that night. Of course, JoAnne didn't come off as the Neighbor Lady, either. Feeney flung a bushel basket of four-letter, Nixonionian expletive-deleteds at her and she parried and returned. Then, to the complete surprise of everyone in the Blackwatch, Joe hopped up on a table, lowered his trousers and-a-one and-a-two and-a-three, he flat out mooned JoAnne.

Needless to say, the conversations in the room dropped several decibels when this change of events occurred. The antics sure put a damper on the good times everyone there was having, and the shocked crowd gradually dispersed.

Time has now transformed that Castle-Feeney incident into a somewhat humorous exchange, I suppose. But had Welk, who at the time was in his declining years, known what took place at the Blackwatch, he may have come down with a sudden and very serious case of old-fashioned apoplexy. Mooning just didn't seem to be Lawrence Welk's style.

12

Ballrooms, Street Dances, and New Year's Eve

There was a time when dance halls of all shapes and sizes dotted the Midwestern landscape. Dancing, before television and the other recreational diversions of today, was a traditional Saturday night event. You could tell a community by the dance hall it kept. The pavilions were assets that brought new people and dollars to a community. The halls were the meccas for Saturday night fun seekers, beckoning music lovers and dancers. Driving fifty or seventy-five miles to dance was not uncommon in the days before television. Many dance halls managed to hang on for a time after television came wafting out to the Midwest. For a time, the two co-existed. I know some people whose Saturday night ritual was to remain at home until after the popular Saturday night show *Gunsmoke* was over, then head for the dance hall or club to complete the evening. The places usually didn't get going until about 9 p.m. anyway, and usually closed about 1 or 2 a.m., depending on local and state laws.

After the dance hall craze subsided in the Midwest by the 1970s, there was a brief period when street dances were the rage. But a litigious society soon began to worry about the responsibilities of those who owned the streets and, in most cases, city councils and community governing boards backed away from approving and granting permits for street dances. Of course, there were street dances while dance halls still flourished, but the sound equipment in the 1950s and 1960s left much to be desired. As sound systems improved, street dances came into their own. A good street dance needs a good sound system to carry for a block or two. That's why I avoided playing for street dances most of the time, until the 1980s.

Most of the dance halls in the upper Midwest were products of the 1920s when dancing was what people did for entertainment and for socializing. Many halls did

111

The Japanese Gardens in Flandreau (SD) City Park, where Myron Lee and the Caddies often played, is one of the best if not the best preserved dance pavilion in the upper Midwest.

double or triple duty, serving as community gathering places and often as roller skating rinks. The dance business thrived, too, during the war years and for a couple of decades following WW II in 1945.

Most of these venerable old palaces are now gone, battered by passing time and the merciless elements. A few dance halls remain, including a beautiful example in Flandreau's City Park called the Japanese Gardens. It had another name during the war with Japan, but was rechristened the Japanese Gardens again when the two countries returned to normal relations. One reason it has survived all of these years is that the residents of Flandreau all have a sense of ownership. It is maintained and supervised with city tax dollars. All through the 1990s, Saturday night dances with live bands were held at the Japanese Gardens.

Nearly all of those early dance halls had excellent dance floors of maple or oak. There was nothing fancy about the actual structures, other than the fact that they were all well built of wood. As a band, we never put much stock in a dance hall's creature comforts, its acoustics, or its ambiance. We judged dance hall venues more by their popularity and the enthusiasm of the people who sought them out.

At or near the very top of my list of dancehall favorites was the Hollyhock Ballroom in Hatfield, MN. A hollyhock, my mother told me, is a hardy flower popular in this area during the 1920s and 1930s, that many old-timers say could survive out here on the flatlands even with conscious neglect. That pretty well sums up the Hollyhock Ballroom at Hatfield. It was hardy and it survived, that's for sure.

Between 1959 and 1965 the Caddies probably played there more than forty times. And nearly every time we managed to pack the place. The little speck of the town of Hatfield had a main street that consisted of a post office, a bar, and nestled up next to it, the old Hollyhock Ballroom. It was a favorite for thousands of people. Crowds at the dances that we were a part of usually were in the neighborhood of 1,000 people.

If you were tall enough to slap your money down on the bar next to the Hollyhock's bar, you could buy a drink. Age wasn't a deciding factor. Every band that could draw a crowd played there at one time or another, including the big time stars like the Everly Brothers, Jerry Lee Lewis, Bobby Vee, Buddy Knox, Conway Twitty, and Tommy Roe. The dressing room was a shoe box of crowded space boarded off in the furnace room. The big stars that played there signed their names on its walls, and we did, too.

Over and above the music and dancing that were the main attractions at the Hollyhock, there were a variety of extracurricular activities. The fisticuffs were

HOLLYHOCK Ballroom

HATFIELD, MINNESOTA

MODERN DANCING

SPECIAL ATTRACTION —
Sat., Feb. 7 .... MYRON LEE
AND HIS CADDIES

Sat., Feb. 14 .... GREG WILT AND
HIS COUNTRY SWING BOYS

Sat., Feb. 21 .... WEDDING DANCE
Jim Albert and Joyce McCorkel
Music by THE AMBASSADORS

Sat., Feb. 28 .... JIMMY THOMAS

OLD TIME DANCING

Thurs., Feb. 5 .... JOLLY
LUMBERJACKS

Thurs., Feb. 12 .... WHOOPEE JOHN

Thurs., Feb. 19 .... SIX FAT
DUTCHMEN

Thurs., Feb. 26 .... BABE WAGNER

This is a poster for the famed Hollyhock Ballroom at Hatfield, MN, from about 1959 or 1960.

The Hollyhock Ballroom in Hatfield, MN, wasn't the prettiest pavilion on the circuit, but it was one of the most popular. Myron Lee and the Caddies played there over fifty times. The Hollyhock burned down and was not rebuilt.

mostly supervised and controlled by a hulking, armed cop properly deputized for duty and hired by personable manager Al Kirby to keep peace and order. Not surprisingly, most of the Hollyhock fights had something to do with a girl. When a fight broke out, the muscular policeman would tuck a fighter under each of his telephone pole sized arms and carry them like sacks of flour to the door. There, he might even encourage them to continue their conflict in the parking lot. We watched all this from the stage, but never missed a beat. Fortunately, no one ever bothered us up on the stage.

    I'm told that once, when the Everly Brothers were at the Hollyhock, a blizzard whipped itself into a raging frenzy. By midnight, the weather was so bad that there was no way anyone at the dance could drive home. Some living nearby tried it and must have made it. But Kirby invited the remaining people to spend the night at his home. The storm continued unabated throughout the next day, but the people who were stranded in Hatfield had a great time. There was plenty to eat and drink and the dance atmosphere continued uninterrupted.

    The Everly Brothers joined in the fun, singing all of their favorite songs with everyone joining in. My friend Lloyd Madison was there that night, and like many others, still remembers that extended dance. I have the same good feelings about the Hollyhock, and all the good times we had there. But fortunately, we never played there during a blizzard. All that remains of the glorious Hollyhock Ballroom today is a cement slab where this wonderful old dance hall once stood.

    I also have many fond memories of playing at the Ruskin Park dance hall. Ruskin Park is and always has been a famous historic landmark in eastern South

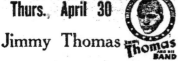

The actual size of this poster announcing the 1959 bookings at the famous Ruskin Park dance hall in Sanborn County was nearly two feet by three feet. Under the listing for Myron Lee and the Caddies, at left, was printed "Featured Attraction: First appearance in this territory..." Myron Lee and the Caddies would later play dozens of times at Ruskin Park.

Dakota along the Jim River in melon country thirty miles northwest of Mitchell near Forestburg. Through the years, all of the popular bands and recording stars stopped at the Ruskin Park dance hall. It was arguably one of the most popular in South Dakota.

Ruskin began in the early 1900s when the farmers who owned the land developed the area into a park for picnics, political rallies, and as community gathering place. At one time it also had an imposing amphitheater, a hotel, and other buildings. The dance hall was built in the 1920s and was a must stop for dances featuring the big bands of the 1930s and 1940s.

In my time, the owners and operators of the dance hall were Walt and Dagmar Seigenthaler. They reluctantly made the transition from big bands to rock and roll and they often hired the Caddies, for which I am forever grateful. During part of the week, incidentally, the dance hall substituted as a popular roller skating rink. When we played there, people came from a wide area to dance, party, and in some cases, fight. As was usually the case, most of the disagreements were over women. But for some reason unique to Ruskin Park, many of the altercations were territorial in nature. It was often some guy who had been too long in the cups, who lived in a larger town, against someone who also had too much to drink, representing a smaller community. They squared off for bragging rights, I guess.

One date we had in 1961 at Ruskin almost didn't happen. I'd checked my date book earlier in the day and mistakenly thought we were scheduled in Leaf Lakes, MN, which is about two hundred miles northeast of Sioux Falls. Ruskin Park is west of Sioux Falls. When we pulled into the Leaf Lake dance hall parking lot early that evening, we were surprised to see another band setting up. I sensed immediately that something wasn't right. I called our booker, Jimmy Thomas in Luverne, MN. He checked his calendar and told me that we were scheduled for Ruskin Park. Fortunately, we had arrived in Leaf Lake early. While Jimmy called Seigenthaler to explain the mix-up, we jumped in the car and took off, leaving a thick plume of Leaf Lake Ballroom parking lot dust in our wake.

Walt Seigenthaler told Jimmy that he expected a big crowd to show up that night. Jimmy assured him we'd be there come hell or high water. The delaying tactic agreed upon was that Walt would explain to the crowd what had happened and keep the people happy by playing recorded music over the sound system until we arrived.

We drove considerably over the speed limit on our over two hundred-mile journey, often reaching eighty or ninety miles an hour if the coast seemed clear. We stopped twice along the way to phone Jimmy and let him know where in our hurried journey we were. Jimmy would then call Ruskin Park with the band's progress. Walt would relay our progress to the crowd.

The Ruskin Park dance always started at 9 p.m. Despite every effort, we didn't get there until about midnight. We pulled in and were amazed that several hundred people were still there waiting for us. They clapped and cheered and we had no difficulty finding enough help to carry our equipment into the dance hall. To make up for lost time and for the loyalty of our fans at Ruskin, we played until about 3 a.m. It was one of the longest nights I can remember.

A year later, in 1962, the Seigenthalers arranged a special mid-week event that featured the Everly Brothers. Walt must not have read the fine print in his contract with the Everlys. He didn't realize that the Everlys only did two forty-five minute shows nightly, not an entire four-hour dance agenda. The Everlys, upon learning that no other group was scheduled despite contractual language to the contrary, dug in their heels, retreating to their fancy touring bus parked among the trees at Ruskin. They threatened to leave because of the possible breach of contract, but agreed to give Walt time to see if something could be worked out. If not, Walt still would have to pay them their $1,500.

Walt, in a panic, called me at home in Sioux Falls about 7 p.m. and explained his dilemma. He told me the place was already packed with people waiting to hear the Everlys, and looking forward to the evening of dancing and drinking. He said the Everlys refused to leave their bus unless he found a band to play between their forty-five minute stints. It was a night off for my band and I had no idea where the guys might be. I told Walt that I would try to locate all of them and check to see if they were willing to help out. Miraculously I was able to find every band member. Each said he would be willing to help Walt and Dagmar out of a difficult situation. I called Walt back within about fifteen minutes. He breathed a sigh of relief and thanked me profusely for our willingness to dig him out.

Ruskin Park is about ninety miles from Sioux Falls. By 10 p.m. we were on stage and rockin'. We had a wonderful time. The crowd was happy. The Everly Brothers were happy. Walt and Dagmar were happy. In fact, Walt was so happy that he even added a little to our paycheck that night. But he must have made out like a bandit, too, because the Everly Brothers attracted a monster crowd. Years later I had an opportunity to remind the Everly Brothers of that night at Ruskin. They remembered, and said they were determined to not leave the sanctity of their bus to try and deal with a disappointed, wild crowd. I'm sure that after that, Walt read every contract in studied detail.

Another memory of Ruskin Park is the night a young lady jumped up on the stage while we were playing and did an impromptu strip tease. Flashing might be a more descriptive word. Apparently she had argued with her date during the evening, and consumed too much of something in the process. Perhaps to make her date jealous, she surprised us all by getting on the stage and pulling her dress up over her head. She was, as everyone could see, wearing only a dress and a smile. The crowd cheered. There was nothing I could do but keep on playing. I imagine there are probably hundreds of people today who were there that night and remember that brief X-rated floor show.

Ruskin Park's dance hall is gone now, but for a century it was synonymous with entertainment and romance. It is still talked about by those who remember the dances there. As do most old dance halls, it had a character of its own. We made a host of friends at Ruskin during the nights we played there.

A fond memory of Ruskin Park is some of the people I met there. Jim and Karen Hoffman, who farm near Artesian, were frequent dancers at Ruskin Park when they were teenagers going together. They were married in 1964, and we played for their wedding dance. I often have hunted on their land, and on Doug and Joyce Olson's land, too, and value the friendships I made in the Artesian area because of our dates at Ruskin Park through the years.

At Ruskin, as we did everywhere, we left our "mark." Jimmy Thomas had little stickers made up by the hundreds. Printed on each was: "Myron was here." We

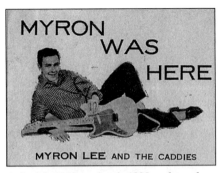

In the late 1950s and early 1960s, a form of advertising was these small sticker "calling cards" that the Caddies pasted up in the venues and the towns they played.

stuck them up everywhere in the ballrooms and other places we visited. They were in the dressing rooms, in gas stations and cafes and, if we arrived early at a dance hall, we'd even stick them in the empty ladies restrooms. I suppose that the Environmental Protection Agency would be on our case today if we fouled the environment in a similar fashion.

West of Ruskin Park was the "repositioned" old Woonsocket dance hall that in 1949 was moved by Andy Pflaum eight miles further west on Highway 34 to the little town of Lane east of Wessington Springs. The dance floor was a gem made of white maple. It was closed for a number of years, but Red and Walter Deneke reopened it in 1963 as the Rainbow Ballroom. We played there many times. Many of the dancers came from Huron. The average attendance was between 300 and 500 people, but I'm told that it mentions in the Lane Centennial Book that the largest crowed ever at the Rainbow was when our band was playing a New Year's Eve dance there. Over 1,200 people showed up.

The dance hall and the attached bar that Pflaum had built when he moved the building over from Woonsocket were separated by a little dividing wall about four feet high. The Rainbow could get slightly raucous at times, but Red and Walt were huge men so no one argued with them as they escorted the troublemakers out the door. The last dance at the Rainbow was the New Year's Eve dance at the end of 1973. I can't remember if we played there that night or not. The historic old Rainbow was torn down in 1974.

Milltown Ballroom, near the site of an old Hutterite flour mill, was another popular summer place that is still remembered by many. Like Ruskin Park, it was also sited on the Jim River north of Yankton. Our agent, Jimmy Thomas, leased the dance hall there for a time during the early 1960s and booked many famous artists for performances there.

One night Jimmy asked me to ride along with him to Milltown. He'd booked a phenomenal triple-header of Jerry Lee Lewis, Conway Twitty, and Gene Pitney, who had just returned to the tour after singing his big hit "Town Without Pity" on the Academy Awards show televised nationally. At the dance hall I tried to make myself useful helping Jimmy prepare for the evening. I remember that Jerry Lee opened the show and did his usual routine of running a big comb through his thick hair and then blowing stealth dandruff out on the crowd. The people who crowded up to the edge of the stage expected it and just loved it.

Conway Twitty followed with a forty-five minute show, singing all of his great hits including one of my favorites, "It's Only Make Believe." After a brief intermission, it was time for Gene Pitney. But Jimmy couldn't find him and asked me to help search him out. We checked the coatroom, the dressing room, the rest-rooms, and other nooks and crannies to no avail.

We grabbed flashlights and headed for the parking lot filled with cars of all makes and models representing several surrounding counties. We walked the lot and checked the cars, calling Pitney's name. Finally, a car door in the back of the lot slowly opened and a somewhat disheveled Pitney emerged, followed by an equally disheveled girl he'd apparently just met. "You're on, you're on," Jimmy informed him. Pitney didn't say a word. He sauntered off toward the hall, button-ing his shirt and running a big comb through his hair as he walked. I stood aside, mouth open, as he passed by.

I remember that the Milltown Dance Hall's stage, probably suffering from old age, slanted, so the mike stand leaned decidedly back toward the person using it. I therefore learned that I had be exceptionally careful at Milltown so I didn't knock out a few front teeth while I was singing.

Tom Archer was a dance hall operator who believed in the economy of scale. He acquired about a dozen ballrooms throughout the Midwest. Over time we played in most of them, including the famous Arkota Ballroom in Sioux Falls, the Shore Acres in Sioux City, and the Valaire Ballroom in Des Moines. Most of Archer's acquisitions had been built in the 1920s and were cavernous, beautiful buildings with large dance floors.

Mag Hansen and his wife Ruth ran the Arkota for Archer for many years. We were often invited to play Teen Hops there on Thursday nights. Mag was a per-fectionist. He took an unusual personal pride in "his" dance floor. Like a brooding mother hen, he was extremely protective of it. We soon learned that it was not good form to carry our band equipment in and walk across the beautiful wood floor to the stage. The correct protocol in Mag's mind was to walk around the edge of the floor to the stage. Whenever the band arrived, he patrolled the area to insure that the proper path was a circuitous one around the dance floor.

In North Dakota, one of our favorite spots, and probably the most unique venue for all of us, was known as Johnson's Barn near Arthur, ND, west of Fargo. As advertised—it was a big barn, complete with the aroma you'd expect in a barn. In fact, it was a dairy barn that still served that purpose. Milk cows chewed their cuds and whiled away the evenings in the lower portion. What had been the hayloft was finished off with a large dance floor and stage. We played there many times, and it was always somewhat disconcerting and humorous for us to be belting out some love song or other, only to have our beautiful renditions punctuated with a burp or a bellow from below, as a bovine either voiced her displeasure with the music, or felt inclined to join in with us.

The first ballroom the Caddies played on our first out-of-town job was the his-toric Groveland Park Ballroom in Tyndall. It has survived the times, but is now a shed on a farm near Tyndall. It started as a dance pavilion in the 1920s at what was called Wonderland Farm, owned by Yankton businessman Fred Donaldson just east of Yankton that later became known as Lakeside Park.

In the 1930s, that round-topped dance pavilion became a part of what was called Green Gables, where Donaldson's son converted the facilities into a resort.

Cabins were built there, and the dance hall flourished. But in 1939, with Green Gables out of favor, W. J. Flamming bought the buildings and moved the pavilion to Tyndall, where it became part of Groveland Park.

The Roof Garden at Lake Okoboji, IA, was an enjoyable venue, as was the Cobblestone Ballroom in Storm Lake, IA. The first time I heard that we were to play at the Cobblestone Ballroom I pictured people dancing around on bricks rather than oak or maple. Junior Lawrence ran the place. When he was drinking, which was frequently, he was a friendly cuss. He'd always insist on buying the band a big steak dinner after closing time. If he happened to be sober, however, we knew there would be no free steaks, and chances are we were in for a dissertation on the high fee we were charging for our services.

That claim, incidentally, wasn't just Lawrence's complaint. Ballroom operators everywhere shared this common opinion. They all seemed to have three very strong opinions and one historical fact about their dance halls. They thought performers charged too much, they sincerely believed their sound systems were the very best, and they were certain that the big band days would return someday and put the rock and roll boys in retreat. The historical fact that applied to every dance-hall around was that Lawrence Welk once played there. Actually, most of the sound systems were usually nearly as old as Mr. Welk, who may or may not have played there. Most of the equipment was the remaining residue from the big band days, right down to those "Shure" microphones big as softballs and the stumpy black speakers standing guard on stage. Those speakers may have served the needs of the big bands, but they were dinosaurs to us.

After we were established and had a little extra cash, I was able to buy my own sound system and carry it with us. My first sound system was an 80-watt Bogen amp from Warren Radio Supply in Sioux Falls. I used two fifteen-inch speakers encased in plywood, one on each side of the stage. After I began using my own equipment, I had to argue with nearly every ballroom operator who was reluctant to have us begin pulling plugs and moving wires and cords around to make room for our system. A few times I had to threaten to pull the band for the night unless we could hook up our own equipment. That always worked.

Minnesota was peppered with dance halls. In the early 1960s we'd often head up old Highway 23 on our way to a job somewhere in the Gopher State. One that I remember well was near New Munich, MN. It was one of our regular stops every six weeks or so. We had a large following in that area and most of our fans showed up when we were there. Erv Schiffler was the New Munich operator. After the dance, when the time came for us to be paid, he invariably had some pointed comments about the fancy new car I was driving. I got the distinct impression that he thought if I could afford the payments on that automobile, he was paying me way too much money.

The Cadillacs or Oldsmobiles I drove were great cars, powerful and capable of bringing out the worst of my driving habits. We were young and felt we would live forever, so speeds of seventy or eighty miles an hour were common. My mom and my agent were always reminding me to slow down. I should have taken their advice. The demise of one of my classy cars came late on a beautiful summer afternoon in 1959. We were merrily on the way to the Little Falls, MN, ballroom, which was about two hundred miles from Sioux Falls. On the way I pulled up behind, and then passed, a rusty old truck loaded with passel of pigs. I breezed by like it was standing still. Unfortunately, I had failed to notice that there was an intersection coming up. Just as we got to the crossing, the farmer turned his pick-up smack into my beautiful car.

It was the end of my station wagon. I remember glancing in the rear-view mirror and watching our equipment trailer fly through the air. It landed in a pasture, along with the rest of us, including the farmer, his pick-up, and his pigs. By some miracle, no one was hurt. However, all four pigs were no longer marketable. The right side of my beautiful car was nearly torn away. The farmer asked why I had passed when he had his left signal light blinking to warn of the turn. We checked the back of his truck and discovered that the wiring to the signal light had worn through, so there was no warning light to see and I was probably spared a traffic citation.

This 1958 Oldsmobile Fiesta wagon was the Caddies' first touring car, bought from Walgraves Motor in Luverne, MN. The new air suspended shocks never worked, and on a trip to a dance in Little Falls, MN, the car was totaled in a collision with a pickup truck loaded with hogs. No one, except hogs, was injured.

A Minnesota highway patrolman took us to a nearby farmhouse and I called Jimmy Thomas. I told him what had happened and asked him to inform the Little Falls ballroom owner of our plight. We'd be a little late. Someone from the ballroom staff came out to get us. We were relieved and pleasantly surprised that the equipment had survived except for a couple of vacuum tubes that had dropped out of our Fender amplifiers. You couldn't hurt those Fender Bassmen amps. They could survive a Force Five hurricane. The ones still around are worth a considerable amount of money. I still have mine. Aside from the hefty construction of the Fender amps, we surmised that the trailer had also been packed so tightly that there wasn't much space in which to bounce around. Later that night, despite a couple of scratches and a few aches and pains, we played the four-hour job at Little Falls as if nothing had happened. In the meantime, Jimmy drove up from Luverne and hauled us, humble and sulking, back home after the dance.

Perhaps one of the most famous ballrooms in the upper Midwest in which we played several times was the Surf Ballroom in Clear Lake, IA. That's where three young giants in the fledgling rock and roll movement played their last show. Of course, I'm speaking of Buddy Holly, Ritchie Valens, and The Big Bopper (J. P. Richardson), who died in the early morning hours of Feb. 3, 1959, when their aircraft crashed near Mason City. They were headed for Moorhead, MN, near Fargo for a concert that evening.

Carole and I had tickets for their appearance scheduled for the Shore Acres Ballroom in Sioux City the next night after their Moorhead show, but of course, they never made it. We drove down anyway and heard Buddy's band, and Dion and Frankie Avalon, who had been flown in as replacements to fill out the show. Whenever we played at the Surf in Clear Lake, our thoughts were with those three lost giants in the music business. Incidentally, Bobby Vee says his big chance came as a result of the Buddy Holly tragedy. The promoters at Moorhead, where Holly and the others were to perform, asked Bobby, who lived in nearby Fargo, to substitute that night, which he did.

Another famous ballroom was the Prom in St. Paul, MN. In 1959, my record "Rona Baby" was on the charts at radio WDGY in Minneapolis. With help from Ki-Ho Helgie mentioned in an earlier chapter, I was invited to a promotional event for the record at the famous Prom Ballroom in St. Paul. Bill Diehl, one of the main DJ's at WDGY, was doing a record hop there that night and the place was packed with over 1,000 young rockers. Jeno's Pizza, a start-up Minnesota company, also had its product introduced at the hop that night. WDGY didn't want my band for the event, which was not uncommon at promos such as this. They just wanted me to come to the Twin Cities and walk out on stage. Diehl would play both sides of my record and I was to do a "lip-sync" of the words. When Diehl introduced me to the audience, the kids, most of whom were teenage girls, yelled and screamed and crowded up close to the stage. I'd seen this phenomena with the big names in rock and roll music, but it was a new experience for me. I liked it.

Lip-syncing and doing the body gyrations, such as they were in those days when compared to the movements of today's stars, were more difficult than I'd imagined. Frankly, I was nervous and worried that I'd make a mistake, but somehow I got through the ordeal. Later, I went to WCCO-TV where I again lip-synced

Myron with popular Minneapolis WDGY radio disc jockey Bill Diehl at the famed Prom Ballroom in St. Paul, MN, during Myron's promotional tour for his song "Rona Baby."

"Rona Baby," this time on Kinescope that the station ran later. Diehl invited me back for other record hops at the Kato Ballroom in Mankato.

This promotional effort was good for me and for the band. From the publicity I received in the Twin Cities area, we picked up many jobs. We worked several clubs in the area, as well as the Excelsior Amusement Park. And through the years we played at many resorts throughout Minnesota. I very much liked the ballroom at Detroit Lakes, but the old and faithful Hollyhock in Hatfield wins my gold medal award.

Although we played in hundreds of dance halls all over the country, the one dance hall that I remember as having a lot of character was in tiny Dimock, SD. The hall was at one time the Dimock State Bank, which closed during the early 1930s. Vic and Hilda Weber purchased the old building in 1957 and transformed it into a popular dance hall. Interestingly, when it was a bank filled with money, it had no security guards on duty. When the Weber's dance hall would get busy in its glory years late in the 1950s and early 1960s, five guards often were hired to watch over the place. I understand that the dance hall was purchased by Don Sudbeck in 1981 and then Javern and Anna Mae Hofer bought it in 1992. It is still going strong, and I commend all of the owners for their efforts to keep the era of the dance hall alive.

Of course, none of the dance halls were air conditioned, but I always thought the dance pavilion on Lake Madison near the city of Madison, SD, had the next best thing. The old pavilion was built in the 1920s right on the shore of the lake. In fact, when it was first built it had boat storage areas on the lower level and the dance hall was on the second floor. The dance hall was built into the side of a hill

This early picture of the Lake Madison Pavilion was provided by pavilion owner Jack Wulf of Lake Madison. The spacious lakeside dance hall with boat houses on the first floor was built in the mid 1920s and burned down in the 1970s. Myron Lee and the Caddies often played there in the 1960s. Upper floor windows could be opened in the summer allowing in cool breezes off the lake.

sloping toward the shore, so people going to the dance entered on the second floor. When we played there, Jack Wulf was the owner. The entire lake side of the hall had huge windows with screens. Jack would open the windows on hot summer nights to catch the breezes off the lake and that helped cool the place down several degrees. Plus, it was a nice view. The beautiful old building burned to the ground in 1975 three years after Jack Wulf sold it.

Street Dances

Maybe it was the gradual demise of the railroad that lit the spark for street dances. As the long-held practice of shipping by rail subsided, semi-trucks began to crowd the highways. And from my long experience with street dances, there isn't a street dance stage that comes even close to matching the portability, size, height, and heft of a flat bed trailer. And a serendipitous result of the proliferation of semi-tractor trailer stages in the Midwest that helped make the production of a street dance so much easier may have been the portable toilet industry.

The street dance goes back for decades in South Dakota and other rural states, but the craze really started to take hold in the mid-1980s. It was a perfect way, even in a town without a paved main street, to bring town residents and young men and women from the surrounding farming community together in a social setting during the warm summer months. Amenities like the rubber-tired stage we used, and a dance floor that might be black top, concrete, grass, or gravel, were common. The crowd could sit on the curb or a lawn chair they brought with them.

And street dances afforded the opportunity for a good fundraising effort for organizations like volunteer fire departments, wildlife groups, political parties, veteran's organizations, the local community club, or chambers of commerce. Since street dance management is labor intensive, groups and organizations had the manpower to handle all of the responsibilities without running up a big expense for help.

By the late 1970s and 1980s, many South Dakota communities were observing their centennial birthdays, and many sponsored a street dance to help in the celebration. But centennial or not, street dances became very popular for a brief time in the last quarter of the last century.

We played in the little town of Artesian every July 3 for years and it was not uncommon there, or at other annual street dances, to meet folks who had followed us as teenagers in the early 1960s. The litany of South Dakota communities where we were privileged to play street dances reads like a state atlas—Montrose, Hartford, Humboldt, White Lake, Kimball, Lennox, Volin, Tripp, Wakonda, Lake Andes, and on and on. I was always surprised at how many people we could attract to a street dance. It wasn't uncommon to have from 3,000 to 5,000 happy people milling around on main street.

The one problem with street dances is the weather. Most of the time, the evenings were wonderful. In Volin one night, a thunder and lightening storm rolled in and threatened to electrocute us en masse before we could get the heck out of there. The town's power failed, the wind blew, and it nearly took us, along with our

Bassman and singer Dave Severtson of the Caddies waves to the crowd at a Fireman's street dance in Dell Rapids in 1989. Over 1,700 attended.

equipment, right off the flat bed trailer. A squadron of tornados had also been reported in the area. Somehow we made it through and got home safely. Surprisingly, our equipment dried out and was ready by the end of the week to work another street dance.

Until portable toilets began to be a part of the street dance scene, people in need had to crowd into bars and pool halls on main street, if there were any, or use their imagination to locate a suitable "necessarium." That all changed, of course, when the ubiquitous port-a-potties came along. At a dance in Garretson one night, I counted twenty-five of them platooned on parade along one side of the street.

On a pre-port-a-potties break at a dance in Humboldt one very, very dark, moonless night, I found what I thought was a private spot behind the flat bed trailer stage. It was a hot night, and I was wearing shorts. As I walked along beside the trailer, I felt a fine spray on my legs. It seems that a young female had also found the darkness under the trailer as a suitable location. Later on, Roger Reynolds, who handled our sound equipment, started driving his motor home to the dances. Then we had a refuge for breaks without tripping over others out behind the truck trailer stage.

In the late 1970s, when the wet t-shirt contests were just gaining popularity, we were exposed, so to speak, to our first such event during a street dance we were playing in Lennox. The contestants came up on stage after having been properly doused. Based on applause after we introduced each young woman individually, a grand champion was selected. It was a more than usual happy, raucous night after that, as I recall. When we were driving away after the dance had ended about 2 a.m., we had to maneuver around and through the main street dance area that was literally covered with a foot of empty beer cans. I understand that the first wet t-shirt contest at that dance was the last in Lennox. And I think it was also the last street dance there, too.

Once, Cliff Highstreet of the Hurley Fire Department asked me about having the band play for a fire department-sponsored street dance there. Hurley's street dances had been getting smaller and smaller crowds and Highstreet knew we had a reputation for bringing in big crowds. But our price of $1,200 scared him away. I remembered that Jimmy Thomas had often employed a percentage inducement for dance hall operators. I called Cliff and offered him a deal. He could guarantee me $500 to cover my band's expenses, or he could pay me sixty percent of the gate, whichever was greater. As a caveat, I told him I would also handle the cost of Hurley Street Dance advertisements on the radio. Cliff agreed to the percentage arrangement. We played the Hurley Street Dance for the next four years and the turnout surpassed my wildest estimates. Thousands of people came by to the tiny Turner County town to hear us.

The first dance we played there was in 1986. I stood on the flat bed trailer stage ready to begin the dance at 9 p.m. From that slightly elevated vantage point in the community's main intersection, I could see the roads leading into town from every direction. I saw nothing but automobile headlights heading our way. By 10 p.m., the two-block downtown area that was cordoned off with snow fencing was packed with people who came from miles around to hear us and to dance.

What amazed me as much as the size of the crowd was the age groups that came to listen and to dance to our music. It wasn't necessarily the older crowd that had grown up with our music. I would estimate that seventy percent of the people were in their twenties and thirties. A good share of the Hurley crowd were college students from Vermillion. The guys in the SAE Fraternity at the University were great supporters of ours. Rock and roll music was making a comeback. Another thing that surprised me was the friendliness of the people. In the early days at dance halls, fights were common occurrences. But at the street dances, I rarely observed conflicts of any kind. Except once. And that was a doozy.

After that first Hurley dance under the percentage of gate arrangement with Cliff Highstreet, I collected sixty percent of the admission cost, which was over $5,000. It was the most I'd ever made for a dance job. Highstreet and the Hurley Volunteer Fire Department were quite pleased, too.

During our fourth annual Hurley appearance in 1990, the warm June weather encouraged what turned out to be the largest crowd ever. If one had counted the coolers the people hauled to town with them, that number would have probably been a Hurley street dance record, too. During the evening, I recognized many people who worked at the *Sioux Falls Argus Leader* newspaper and also some folks from KELO television out dancing in the street. At midnight, we returned to the stage after our break for the final hour of music. We always saved some of our best crowd pleasers for our final set.

At about 12:15, we suddenly lost electrical power. Everything went dark on stage. In fact, everything went dark in Hurley. A transformer had failed. Fortunately, there was a full moon. I could still see the thousands of people in the crowd. They were staring up at us, wondering why our music had suddenly stopped. A few moments

Dave Severtson and Myron Lee at a street dance in Flandreau, SD. Note the Crystal Theater marquee in the background, left. Townspeople had the old theater refurbished to its 1940s and 1950s glory, and it is now a Flandreau gem.

later I noticed a slight scuffle off to the side. Other clusters of people were beginning to act a little surly, too. From my experience at "crowd watching" from the stage, I knew the situation was getting dicey. The small fight off to the side near where Roger and Arlene Reynolds and our sound equipment were stationed soon erupted into a full-fledged brawl. I was pleased to see that several SAE members from Vermillion were pitching in to help Roger protect our equipment from the fighters. Hurley's cop was on duty, but the situation was way beyond anything he could control. I still had hope that some semblance of reason would prevail. There were now several people on the roof of a building across the street from the stage tossing beer bottles down on the crowd. I could hear the glass breaking. With the electricity out, I had no way of using the microphones to help calm the milling crowd.

Within a few minutes, in hopes of breaking up the melee, the Hurley firemen rolled out their fire truck and drove it slowly into the crowd, spraying water from the truck's tank at anyone who wasn't moving. Some people who took direct hits with the water stream were knocked to the pavement. The firemen had the right idea, but it didn't work. What had been an enjoyable, happy time for everyone had now become a dangerous mob scene. People who weren't fighting or throwing beer bottles were sprinting to their cars or rushing for cover. The dance was ending in chaos.

Of course, with an abundance of reporters from the *Argus Leader* and the KELO newsroom in attendance, the event could not be ignored. The next day, news stories told about the riot in Hurley, where "Myron Lee and the Caddies were playing." It went out on the Associated Press wires, too, getting even wider coverage. Word spread to the small towns where street dances were popular. The attitude and approach to street dance sponsorship changed, perhaps because of the Hurley experience and similar outbreaks at other towns. City boards and councils, when they were asked to approve of a street dance, began to think about what their legal responsibilities were. Sponsors, too, stepped back to think about the legal ramifications. Main street businessmen and women worried about insurance premiums on big plate glass windows going up. I also think that perhaps since our band was at the Hurley event, we received an undeserved rap for "attracting" large crowds of troublemakers and unruly crowds. Our bookings for street dances declined, as they did for every other band. But so did the number of street dances.

While some communities still have them, the tradition of summer outdoor dances ended.

New Year's Eve Parties

During my thirty-four years in the business, I only missed playing at two New Year's Eve dances. The first was in 1959. We were scheduled to play in Alexandria, SD, but as we drove to the event, the weather worsened. By the time we got to Alexandria, we were in the midst of a raging blizzard. The dance was cancelled, so we unwisely elected to drive back to Sioux Falls. We barely made it.

The second missed New Year's Eve was one for which I purposely didn't book any dance. I was curious about what it was like to actually join the crowd for the year end celebration, so decided to try it. It must not have been all that great, because I never took time off again on that special celebration.

After a good run at Sir Richards in Sioux Falls, I got a call and a good money offer from the manager of what is now the Ramkota Hotel who wanted us for a New Year's Eve dance there. The band spent nine New Year's Eves playing at the Ramkota, and the crowds got bigger every year.

For the ninth New Year's Eve, I arranged for about twenty of my good friends and relatives from Yankton to attend the dance. I asked that a block of good rooms be set aside for them, and that they be seated together up front near the dance floor and the stage.

But when we arrived for the event, I learned that not only were my invited guests seated in the rear of the large convention center, but their rooms were not in a block at all, but were scattered throughout the hotel. I'd told them all of my plans, and I was embarrassed that my request to the manager had not been honored.

I'm usually understanding and not easily upset, but when I learned that my reservations had not been honored I turned red with rage. I looked up the manager. He told me that his job was not to cater to the band or to my relatives, but to serve all of the people.

I asked him if he realized who was drawing all of the people to his precious hotel on New Year's Eve in the first place. I was tempted to add that the band would be leaving the place as soon as we could tear down our equipment. But I just couldn't back out because there were hundreds of people who had driven out to dance and to hear our music.

Well-known South Dakota newspaper reporter and columnist Terry Woster still has a big poster of Myron Lee and the Caddies hanging in his Pierre office, along with pictures of James Dean and Johnny Cash. He's Pierre Bureau chief for the Sioux Falls Argus Leader and was at a Fireman's Dance at the Ramada Inn in Pierre in 1991. Myron, right, convinced him to come on stage and sing his rendition of "Jailhouse Rock." Lee remembered an earlier column Woster had written about he and his date (his future wife Nancy) attending a Myron Lee and the Caddies dance in Gregory, SD. "It was a magical night for us," Woster said. "Curtis Powell was The Caddies' lead player then. He had a big Gretsch hollow-body electric. He was as good a guitar player as I've ever heard."

I continued to steam throughout the dance. Afterwards, as we packed up to leave, I told the manager we wouldn't be back. The very next morning I walked across the way and talked to the manager of the adjacent Howard Johnson Hotel. I asked him if he would be interested in booking my band for the following New Year's Eve. He said he certainly would, and offered his large convention center to me free of charge. I could sell the tickets and keep the profit. His business would benefit from the people who elected to have dinner and stay over that night.

We went on to sell the Howard Johnson out every New Year's Eve for eight years. The first year at our new location, I made it a point to check the parking lots of the two hotels. The one we were playing at was chock full. The Ramkota lot was nearly empty. I hoped that the same manager was still there, looking out the window at me looking at him.

By 1992, the lure of the New Year's Eve dance began to fade. There were more house parties, and the desirable positive efforts to reduce drinking and driving were impacting the big dances and celebrations. I've often assumed that the dropping of that neon-lite ball on Times Square that is televised throughout the nation also kept the people away from the public New Year's eve parties. A variety of changes were impacting the traditional celebrations so the crowds were smaller and the people who came seemed to leave the dance earlier. The business as I knew it during my career had changed. We decided to try celebrating the end of the year like everyone else. We never played a New Year's Eve dance again.

13

The Last Dance

The dogs, panting and darting before us, didn't like it, and we weren't all that happy, either. We were in a great pheasant hunting area, but now, four weeks into the season, the pheasants were wild and skittering to safety far ahead of us. The only things our faithful hunting dogs were picking up were bellies and tails full of sandburs, some spilling down and covering their legs and paws. It was a great year for sandburs, if not for pheasants.

It was November 9, 1992, and Bud Thoms and I were walking our usual hunting routes on the Jim and Karen Hoffman farm near Artesian in Sanborn County, not far from the old Ruskin Park Pavilion where the band had played dozens of times. The land we walked belonged to a couple that, as teenagers and later as newlyweds, had attended some of those dances at Ruskin Park. We also played some street dances in their home town of Artesian, so I became friends with them and watched their family grow. They, and their neighbors Doug and Joyce Olson, have always been kind and allowed us to hunt on their land.

We walked back to our pickup truck after our unsuccessful tromp through a usually productive shelterbelt. With our shotguns shouldered, Bud and I began talking and complaining about how bad the hunting and the sandburs and the weather were. That led to a discussion on how times were changing. We were getting older. Bud had me by twenty years, but we both agreed that nothing seemed to be the same anymore. Bud, a well-known hunter who has probably walked more South Dakota fields than anyone I know, talked about his days as a kid in the late 1940s, hunting the fields of South Dakota that were literally awash with plump pheasants. He mentioned several of those childhood hunts, and how much fun it had been. Then suddenly, he stopped in his tracks and just stood there, looking at the ground, deep in thought. I wondered with concern if perhaps the strenuous trek through the shelterbelt had worn him out. I asked him what was wrong.

131

"They're gone, Myron, they're all gone, the good days are all gone," he answered, looking up at me. "And you know what I've just decided? I'm quitting this darn hunting business for good. This is the last time."

We continued our walk back to the pickup in silence, broke down our guns, loaded the tired, burr-infested dogs in the back and drove off. We'd clean them up later.

I knew Bud was frustrated, and on the way back to Sioux Falls I thought about his sudden epiphany. I knew exactly what he was saying and I understood exactly how he felt. I'd been spending much of my time lately thinking about the good old days of the band and the way music and the music business had been then. Thinking back now, I guess it was during that ride back to Sioux Falls, after Bud's last hunt, that I, too, started looking at my options. I'd seen the best of times and I knew they weren't coming back. I wasn't all that encouraged by what I was seeing for the future of my kind of business.

In the days after rock and roll music just seemed to stop in its tracks as the Beatles craze worked itself out in the 1960s and 1970s, and when I had to find real work to support my family, I had still tried to keep the band together. And gradually, with the Sir Richard's job finally coming my way, and with others that followed, plus what seemed like the public's re-acceptance of the very danceable rock and roll music, we were busy again. We were riding high as a local and area favorite, and my black appointment book was no longer gathering cobwebs.

I'd been able to hire Roger Reynolds and his wife Arlene to help with the driving duties as well as our growing inventory of sound equipment and lighting equipment. Without Roger and Arlene's help over many years, I doubt if I would have kept the band together so long. With this technical help, our little group had grown to six. I continued with the rhythm guitar and sang. Dave Severtson was our bassman. Rick Burkhart was on guitar and Gary Swanson was our drummer and—as a non-drinker—our designated driver on our long trips home. We were a team again busy with regular work doing what we loved to do. The good times were back.

With the good times came new technology. I now had a new tandem trailer that was packed with electronic devices for sound enhancement and for lighting. This was good and it was also bad. Often, with all six of us pitching in to set up, the procedure to carry in and set up all of the paraphernalia required an hour and a half, or nine man-hours. And it took just as long to tear all of it down at the end of the night. I thought that the investment of eighteen man-hours of work seemed excessive for the value of all that fancy stuff. But changing times had dictated its use. I remember that fitting all of that equipment into the trailer was like putting a puzzle together. I often compared working with a band to those roustabouts working with the Barnum and Bailey Circus that I watched perform in my early years in Sioux Falls. Only we didn't have elephants for the heavy lifting. Fortunately for me, I was the oldest "elephant" in the herd by five or ten years, so the others would often take pity and give me the easiest unloading and loading tasks. And I think they sensed that the constant grind and routine and long hours were beginning to wear on me. They worked hard to make me feel younger and to have fun, and I'm grateful that they usually succeeded.

The Caddies and long-time sound man Roger Reynolds, in t-shirt at left, pose with Roger's infamous "health drink" sited reverently in the mayonnaise jar on the stool. The band called the brew "brain damage." Roger used his own version of a Black Russian recipe and brewed the mixture at home. At dates the band played where liquor wasn't sold, he tucked it under his arm and brought it in, telling anyone who asked that it was a "health drink" he needed. From left, Gary Swanson, Reynolds, Rick Burkhardt, Dave Severtson, and Myron.

Everything was relatively new to them, but it was a series of mostly reruns for me. The places where we played were new to all of them, but I'd been there and done that dozens of times. Some places, I'd played fifty times or more.

One of our traditions, once we'd loaded up the tandem trailer and were homeward bound after a dance, was to fill our bellies with drink and food. We knew the location of every all-night grocery store in a five-state area. It would be 2 or 3 a.m.

At a country-western dance in 1978, the band wore appropriate attire, from left, Mike Holm, Rick Burkhardt, Gary Swanson, and Myron Lee, kneeling.

when we pulled into a store somewhere, and stocked up on our favorite goodies. Sometimes, our circuitous trip to the store would actually add miles to the journey home, but none of us had eaten for eight to twelve hours, so the post-performance feast was worth the wait and the miles.

We loaded up on bread, cold cuts, cheeses, Miracle Whip, and all of the other staples qualifying because of their high calorie count. My favorite was, and still is, a huge chunk of Morrell's Cervelot. Roger Reynolds was in charge of making the sandwiches, as drummer Gary Swanson herded our big van home. The tape player was loaded with our favorite songs and we all joined in as we lumbered along with that big tandem trailer following us back to Sioux Falls. I think musicians are the only people who can understand the camaraderie that exists between those of us who played the dance circuit. We were in another world when we were out on the road. The real world was left in Sioux Falls. It's a lot like being a kid again. The adrenalin rush and the excitement of the music throbbing through your head gives you just a wonderful feeling. It is such a high that many in the business never quit because of what it does for them. It often leads to other substitutes for those natural highs, too.

I am thankful that in my thirty-four years on the road, I didn't succumb in any habitual way to the temptations of liquor, drugs, the distractions and the flotsam and jetsam of the business. I credit Carole with helping to keep my head on straight and my eyes on the road. Being married to a musician might be the most difficult job in the world. Carole passed the test with flying colors.

On one those long trips through the middle of the night, with a big triple deck sandwich dripping Miracle Whip on my lap, I started thinking more and more about my hunting partner Bud Thoms and the business I was in that was changing

One of the band's last jobs in 1992 at the Westroads Casino in Sioux Falls. From left, Dave Severtson, Myron, and Dick Dawson, right. Drummer Gary Swanson is in the back.

faster than I was able to adjust. The music was becoming more rebellious and irreverent. Many of the artists were working harder and harder to create shock and awe for the demanding audiences. Gimmicks having nothing to do with music seemed to be attracting the fans. Laser beams and fireworks, smoke, and gaudy, clown-like makeup and wild, bare-in-places costumes were becoming more a part of the music of the 1970s and 1980s. Facial hardware was being stuck here and there and becoming more common. The more obnoxious and profane the artist, it seemed, the more popular he or she might become. There were times when I thought it would be so much easier to be back with just my 80 watt Bogen amp, two speakers, and a couple of colored flood lights like when we started long ago out at the Stardust.

And I would ask myself: what in the world will the music business in the 1990s and the next century be like? Did I want to be a part of it? Certainly not the part that required laser beams, nose rings, and smoke bombs. For one thing, I didn't think that should be a part of music. For another, we didn't have room in our tandem trailer for it all.

The busiest year ever for me, despite these changes in the national music scene, was 1989. I was making more money than I'd ever made before. There was an accumulation of fans that had been attracted to the band for over thirty years. Although older now, they still yearned to dance to the Caddies music of old. And rock and roll music was coming back into the lives of many younger people, too.

Then, in 1992, just three years later, the bottom again fell out of my little niche in the music business. A new cycle of music preference had elbowed in. New attitudes were emerging, not just in music in the upper Midwest, but in all aspects of American culture, all across America. The dance craze was ending. Raucous par-

Myron Lee shortly after his retirement in 1992.

tying and exhibition drinking came stumbling in. Where once people at dance halls and lounges may have imbibed a bit, and danced a lot, now the dance part was playing second fiddle, if part of the Saturday night at all.

All through the good days of the big bands and the rock and roll era, a large segment of those who went out for an evening of dancing actually spent the entire evening dancing and having a good time. There would be drinking, of course, but it was limited for the most part. Dances once started at 9 p.m. and continued until midnight or 1 a.m. Most people stayed at the dance hall or lounge until the end.

But as the flavor of ice cream has gone from just vanilla to one hundred and one choices, so, too, were there many other entertainment choices and diversions, from television to movies on video tape to video-lottery machines and a plethora of other events intended to entertain. Dancing is now just one of one hundred and one choices. Even the form of dancing has changed from a synchronized movement matching the music's beat to a discombobulated series of arm waving, shoulder turning, hip pumping, and a swaying kind of herky-jerky movement that hardly resembles actual dancing at all.

Another societal change, and a positive one, I believe, is the success of the drinking and driving efforts. In my growing up years, alcohol caused horrendous accidents. It still does, but not in the comparative numbers that it did in the 1950s and 1960s. The successful efforts to discourage drinking and driving may not have reduced per capita alcohol consumption, but it certainly has moved the site for consumption from the more public places such as dancehalls, Elks lodges, and similar venues, to private parties and homes catering to a small group of people where better reason may prevail.

Adding to the decline and fall of the music that I played are legal issues that are now more prevalent. There was a time when the band was hired for just about every convention that came to Sioux Falls. Christmas parties also kept us busy. It wasn't unusual for us to be booked for twenty of the thirty-one days in December. We played the KELO Christmas party for twelve years in a row and were also invited to play for the parties sponsored by Sunshine Groceries, Midland National Life, and Schwan's, to name a few.

But gradually, like the street dance, this tradition began to change. Companies became concerned about their liability for their employees after they left the parties at which liquor was served compliments of the boss. As a result, companies made adjustments in their party's format. The type and length of the party was changed. I observed this phenomenon at the dances and events we played. People began to leave the premises earlier and earlier. In the old days, people would dance and stay to the bitter end. Now, after our first break at 10 p.m. or so, about half the crowd would depart, either for other entertainment venues, or for home. In 1989, South Dakotans voted to allow video lottery, another diversion from dancing, but a good thing for the bar and lounge owners who were losing the same customers dance bands were.

As the scene changed, so did I.

In November of 1992, a month or so after I returned from the Artesian pheasant hunt with Bud Thoms, I decided that the things that I had seen I could see no more. I would retire from the music business.

I talked to the members of the band about my decision about a month before our last job, which was to be the Vern Eide Christmas party. They were disappointed for me and saddened that I'd be leaving, but I think they had seen over the past couple of years the changes that I was experiencing. It was hard to face them all. We'd been through a lot. Roger and Arlene Reynolds had been with me for twenty-five years. Rick Burkhardt was a faithful compatriot for seventeen years, and Gary Swanson, our driver and drummer, had put up with me for twelve years.

When Rick Burkhardt decided to leave the band after all of our years together, it was like the final nail in the coffin for me. He had been such a great help and a loyal friend, always there through thick and thin. Dick Dawson was Rick's successor, and a wonderful player, too. But by this time I was making up my mind to set aside my guitar.

The day of the Vern Eide party wasn't much different than others. We hauled in all of that fancy equipment from our tandem trailer, and set up as we had so many times before. The folks at KELO-TV had gotten word that this would be my swan song, and a reporter and cameraman came by for an interview to be aired that evening during the 10 p.m. news.

Right on time, at 9 p.m., the band started the evening. We played through the selections as we had so many times before and I sang and played songs that had been a part of me since I started thirty-four years ago, appearing on stages from one coast to the other. During the evening, I noticed that Linda and Duane Krumbach, who had been present at so many of our dances through the years, were happily swaying out there in front of the stage. At midnight, I took a brief moment to thank everyone at Vern Eide and all those at the party for having us as their guests, then I stepped back from the microphone to begin our last song.

Before we could start, Linda Krumbach walked up to me. She had tears in her eyes and some streamed down her face. She asked me if for our last song we could play one of her all-time Caddies favorites.

I'd managed to remain composed and in control during the evening. But when Linda came forward and made her request, I lost it. As we began to play her favorite, "Peter Rabbit," the song I'd done in every job I'd had since 1961 when we first recorded it, the impact of what was happening finally hit home. This would be the last time I'd ever do this. A lump came to my throat and it was difficult to finish the song.

Then it ended and everyone began to clear the room. I set my guitar down and all of us in the band were quiet and red-eyed. We couldn't look at one another for fear we'd break out and cry. We silently put together our tandem trailer puzzle as we had done so many times before. I closed the trailer door, snapped the lock shut, and it was over.

When I got home that night I sat alone in the dark in my kitchen and thought about all of the years of coming home in the early-morning hours. Scenes flashed before me, tumbling by in a rush. I saw that old upright that my dad and I played on. I remembered the St. Mary's Catholic Church cemetery when I was just eight years old. I shivered again as I relived the wonderful Canadian Tour with Buddy Knox. I thought of Bobby Vee, of our friendship and how much he had helped me realize my dream. I remembered the sound of gunfire that echoed through Dallas and America, and Air Force One doing that slow, sad banking turn toward Washington. I smiled as I remembered the night I had a memorable breakfast with a caravan of talented stars.

And I remembered when I was seventeen and Mom had to sign my contract with Jimmy Thomas. It was an agreement covering five long years. I never dreamed then that I'd be part of the music business anywhere near that long. But now, nearly three and one-half decades, hundreds of thousands of miles, and thousands of friends later, it was over.

It had been a wonderful trip.

Epilogue

It's been nearly twelve years since I packed the guitar away in the closet under our stairs, and started living a normal life during the sunny part of the day. After I folded up the band and stepped away, people would invariably ask—and still do—if I missed the business. It's a fair question to someone who has abandoned a wonderful career.

But without hesitation I can honestly say that no, I don't miss it in the least. I think, with all the changes in the business I've discussed in the preceding chapters, I experienced a severe case of burn out. I feel it each day even now. Most musicians never go at the pace I kept, non-stop, day after day, year after year, for thirty-four years. And the travel was numbing, with most of the trips in the dark of night before the Interstate Highway system simplified automobile travel.

For the first year after I retired, I enjoyed being able to do the normal things husbands and wives and families do. There were dinners out with Carole, movies, time with friends, and going to dances to listen to other groups providing the music, or sitting at home with a big bowl of popcorn. Each time when out on the town, there was a comfortable feeling that we could actually get up and leave the place whenever we wanted to. We weren't stuck there bound by some written contract until 1 a.m. or whatever time was legally stipulated. And there was no packing up the trailer and driving back to Sioux Falls through all kinds of weather at all hours of the night.

I noticed that when Carole and I stayed at home on a Saturday night, I'd glance at my watch around 9 p.m. and feel as if it was time to start the dance somewhere out there.

A good friend, Dave Rowe, who for many years had been in the business as a disc jockey, suggested that since I had all that good sound equipment gathering dust in my garage, why didn't I put it to use as a disc jockey playing songs at dances and other events. I told him I wasn't really interested, but I started thinking about it and called him back in a day or two. He helped me change my equipment over to this new use. Now, I'd be playing CD's, not a guitar. After a few jobs, I found that I liked what I was doing.

Soon, offers for jobs at weddings, parties, and dances were streaming in. Working this way rather than with a band was so much easier. I had only myself and my equipment to worry about. But even manhandling my equipment was hard work, so I hired Duane Krumbach to go with me. He'd help with the heavy lifting, he did the driving, and he was just good company along the way.

I've always had a good "feel" for the audiences. With my experience on the stage since I was a pup, I can pretty well "read" the crowds. So it was a piece of cake for me to select the music the people at any particular event seemed to prefer. I found that after the party, I had the same good feeling of knowing that I'd helped hundreds of people enjoy themselves, as I had when I was fronting for my band.

And after all, what I've always been more than anything else was a band leader. I never considered myself as having been blessed with anything more than an aver-

Myron as a DJ doing a class reunion party at Cedar Shores in Chamberlain in 1995. He still does DJ work on a limited basis, and enjoys sharing the music with his audiences.

age singing voice, and I had only an average talent with the guitar. But what I believe I was best at was being a good businessman and a good manager of musicians. My desire throughout my career was always to play music the people wanted to hear. I was also blessed—or very lucky—with gathering good talent around me for my band. I believe that I had some of the greatest musicians one could ask for. They made me look good.

I suppose there are some musicians out there who feel that I have "sold out" by becoming a DJ. But they don't know what makes me tick. Duane and I have had fun with this new venture for about ten years now. Four or five years ago we were doing a wedding dance at the Sioux Falls Holiday Inn. Barney Fritch, a retired minister of my First Lutheran Church, was there. We had time to visit and I asked him if he had married the bride and groom in whose honor the party was being held.

"Heavens no," he said. "I'm here as a friend of the family. I don't do weddings and I don't do funerals anymore." He said he did that all of his life and he enjoyed serving in the ministry, but now that he was retired, "that was it."

I found myself nodding in agreement and knowing exactly what Rev. Fritch was saying.

I don't know how long I will continue with the DJ business. I'm older and I find I get tired earlier. In fact, the event I may be working now often starts about the time I normally hit the hay. Maybe I need to move to Sun City, AZ, and be a DJ there. They start dancing at 6 p.m. and quit by 9 p.m. That would more perfectly fit my lifestyle.

From time to time I get calls for people asking me to get the old band together just one more time for old time's sake. Once I was offered a large sum of money to do just that. The event would take place at the South Dakota State Fair. But without even thinking about it, my answer was no thank you. The analogy of the aging boxer or athlete in any other sport trying a comeback comes to mind.

There was a time and a place for Myron Lee and the the Caddies. And quite a time it was. But now, that's passed by and is no more.

I'm so grateful that so many people have fond memories of Myron Lee and the Caddies. Memories are often much better than the real thing.

Caddies through the Years

Drums

Greg Hall
Dick Robinson
Dick Davie
Chico Hajek**
Stu Perry****
Jerry Kroon*****
Marc Wroe*
Gayland Bender
Bobby Berge
Don Bourret †
Rich Stevenson
Chuck Spawn
Jay Hardy
Greg Olsen
Gary Swanson

*Marc Wroe died in 2002
**Chico Hajek moved to Los Angeles in the late 1960s and became a scene painter artist for NBC television. He worked the background scenes for the Dean Martin TV shows and for many of the Johnny Carson television shows.
****Stu Perry was the drummer in the movie The Posiden Adventure. He is now a drummer in clubs in New Orleans.
*****Jerry Kroon is now a studio drummer in Nashville, TN.
† In the 1960s, Don Bourret was the drummer for the famous band out of Sioux City called the Velaires. They had the hit record "Roll Over Beethoven" that was in the Top Forty.

Guitar

Curt Powell*
Randy Charles
Ron Neuberger
Archie Jenkins
Steve Sandness
Rick Burkhardt
Dick Dawson

*Curt Powell died of cancer in 2004.

Bass

Jerry Haacke
Greg Weeg
Daryl Hoiland
Gordon Underwood
Bob Varns
Dwight Goheen
Mike Holm
Dave Severtson

Sax

Barry Andrews*
Fred Scott
Bob Keys***
Jim Axelson****
Cal Arthur
Joel Shapiro

*Barry Andrews died in the 1960s.
***Bob Keys has been with the Rolling Stones for the past twenty-five years.
****Jim Axelson also played trumpet.

A Veteran Caddie Remembers

By Rick Burkhardt

I first met Myron Lee in the fall of 1968. I was attending Augustana College in Sioux Falls on a football scholarship. Because I played in my high school band and had a rock and roll band for most of my high school years, I was interested in playing in college as well. I met some local players and asked them about any guitar gigs available in town. I was told Myron Lee was in need of a lead guitarist. So I called him and he hired me for a short time until Ron Neuberger, his regular lead player, decided to move back from Minneapolis after about a month there.

Little did I know that about seven years later he would need a long-term player. During the seven year hiatus, I played with some college friends in a band called "Steel Blue" that briefly included Mike Miller, a well-known guitarist and live artist now on the West Coast.

I was also in a group known as "The Fabulous Talisman" for almost five years before Myron called and said he needed a bass player. When I learned songs, I always learned both lead and bass parts, so switching to bass wasn't a problem. I started out my long-term stay in the Caddies playing bass. A few months later Ron Neuberger left again for Minneapolis, for good this time, so I switched back to lead guitar for the last sixteen years with the band. We had some good bass players after I switched to lead guitar, including Dwight Goheen, Mike Holm, and lastly, a reunion with one of the bass players from the Talisman, Dave Severtson.

In the late 1970s we started to play for quite a few fundraisers for fire departments and civic groups. We were a good draw in those years. We could be counted on to draw anywhere from 1,500 to 10,000 people. Interestingly, it was a firemen's dance in Trent, SD, where I met my future wife, Kay. We got married nine months later and so far, twenty years later, we're still together with three great kids.

There were some fun people in the band in my years with the Caddies, and we also met a lot of good people along the way. There are road stories that all musicians have and we were no exception. They are much too numerous to even mention. Needless to say, we had some wonderful times and made a lot of folks happy. The 50s, 60s, and 70s music we specialized in was and still is the best dance music ever. I often wish we were still active on the local music scene because we were the best around at that genre during those years. Myron and I shared the idea that the music should be fun and I think that helped make us successful.

Myron Lee and the Caddies were inducted into the Iowa Rock and Roll Hall of Fame at Arnold's Park, Iowa, in September 2001. Myron invited Curt Powell, as the Caddie's first lead guitarist, and me, as the last, to accompany him to the event.

In September 2001, Myron Lee, right, was inducted into the Iowa Rock and Roll Hall of Fame during ceremonies at Arnold's Park. Myron was accompanied to the event by his first lead guitarist, the late Curt Powell, left, and Rick Burkhardt, center, who was the band's last lead guitarist. Jerry Haacke was invited along, too, but could not attend. Burkhardt was with the band for seventeen years. Myron was also inducted into the Rockabilly Hall of Fame of Minnesota, in December 1999.

It was a proud moment for me and a great memory of my rock and roll years. Although I was only a fan at the beginning of the rock and roll era, it was with much enjoyment that I later played the music.

Musicians like Myron made it possible for a large number of people to enjoy music. From his regional hit singles like "Peter Rabbit," "Rona Baby," "Town Girl," and "Everybody's Goin' to The Party," to the Dick Clark Caravan of Stars tours, he did it all. He made life fun for music fans, and during my years with the band, we had a ball. Those times can never be duplicated.

Myron Lee Discography

45 rpm records

"Homicide"/"Aw C'mon Baby"
Hep 2146
1958

"Rona Baby"/"To Be Alone"
Hep 2076
1958

"Rona Baby"/"To Be Alone"
Felsted 8570
1958

"Mary's Swingin' Lamb"/"Oh Janie"*
Soma 1114
1959

"Baby Sittin'"/"Come Back Baby"
Keen 82104
1960

"Lover's Holiday"/"Magic In a
Summer Night"
Hep 2102
1960

"Blue Lawdy Blue"/"I Need
Someone"
Nor-Va-Jac 1326
1960

"Blue Lawdy Blue"/"I Need Someone"
Quality 1308
1960

"Someone I Know"/"From Now On"
Jaro-J 77037
1961

"Peter Rabbit"/"A Fella Needs a Girl"
M&L 1004
1962

"Town Girl"/"School's Out"
Del-Fi 4180
1962

"Fat Man"/"Summertime Blues"
Garrett 4009
1963

"Everybody's Going to the
Party"/"Honky Tonk Song"
ABC 10610
1965

*This record had Myron's picture on
the label. It was the first time a photograph of the artist was printed as part
of the label, and thus it has become a
collectors record.

Albums

Myron Lee and the Caddies
"Rock and Roll Midwest Style"
Released 1980 in Europe

Myron Lee and the Caddies
"Then and Now"
Early 1980s

Myron Lee and the Caddies
"Still Packin' 'Em In"
1986

Compact Disc

Myron Lee
"Rockin' and Rollin': Out of the
Midwest"
Released in Europe
Collector Records CLED 4439
1998

1963 & 1965 Dick Clark Caravan of Stars Tour Schedule

1963

Nov. 8—Teaneck, NJ
Nov. 9—Utica, NY
Nov. 10—Hartford, Conn.
Nov. 11—Scranton, Penn
Nov. 12—Johnstown, Penn.
Nov. 13—Huntington, W. Va.
Nov. 14—Charleston, W. Va.
Nov. 15—Cincinnati, Oh.
Nov. 16—Evansville, Ind.
Nov. 17—Elkhart, Ind.
Nov. 18—Madison, Wis.
Nov. 19—Davenport, Ia.
Nov. 20—Sioux City, Ia.
Nov. 21—Wichita, Kan.
Nov. 22—Dallas, Tx.
Nov. 23—Oklahoma City, Ok.
Nov. 24—St. Louis, Mo.
Nov. 25—Nashville, Tenn.
Nov. 27—Louisville, Ky.
Nov. 28—Pittsburgh, Penn.
Dec. 1—Richmond, Va.
Dec. 2—Winston-Salem, NC
Dec. 3—Knoxville, Tenn.
Dec. 5—Charlotte, NC
Dec. 6—Raleigh, NC
Dec. 7—Norfolk, Va.

1965

April 29—Rehearse in New York City
April 30—Open tour in Johnstown, Pa.
May 1—Philadelphia, Pa *(Rolling Stones joined us for this show)*

May 2—Bluefield, W. Va
May 3—Pikeville, Ky.
May 4—Richmond, Ky.
May 5—McComb, Ill.
May 6—Paducka, Ky.
May 7—Muncie, Ind.
May 8—Vincennes, Ind.
May 9—Ashland, Ky.
May 10—Clarkville, Tn.
May 11—Atlanta, Ga.
May 12—Charleston, SC
May 13—Jacksonville, Fla.
May 14—Mobil, Ala.
May 15—Columbus, Ga.
May 16—Panama City, Fla.
May 17—Macon, Ga.
May 18—Augusta, Ga.
May 19—Columbia, SC
May 20—Open
May 21—Winston Salem, NC
May22—Charleston, W. Va.
May 23—Erie, Pa.
May 24—Pittsburgh, Pa.
May 25—Syracuse, NY
May 26—Wochester, Mass
May 27—Troy, NY
May 28—Hershey, Pa.
May 29—New Haven, Conn.
May 30—Hartford, Conn.
May 31—Utica, NY
June 1—Ottowa, Canada

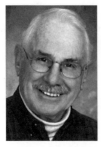 Chuck Cecil is a native South Dakotan. He was born in Wessington Springs and grew up in Rapid City. After serving as an aerial photographer in the Navy during the Korean War, he enrolled at South Dakota State University where he earned bachelor's and master's degrees in journalism. After a decade in the newspaper business, he joined the university and served in various editorial capacities and then as assistant to the president until he took early retirement to establish a chain of ten weekly newspapers along the I-29 corridor through four eastern South Dakota counties. He retired in 2000 and now does freelance writing. He has written eight books and continues to write a column in the *Brookings (SD) Daily Register*. His books are *Stubble Mulch, Pony Hills, Becoming Someplace Special—The Brookings Story, Remember The Time, The RFD News, Family Matters, You Can Bank On It—The BANKFIRST STORY, The Brookings Album*, and *Myron Lee and the Caddies: Rockin' 'n Rollin' Out of the Midwest.*